I0568312

Circular Knitting Handbook

A Definitive Guide to Learn How to Knit in the
Round Plus Patterns, Accessories, and Knitting
Tools to Get You Started

By

Zera Meyer

Disclaimer

This publication is designed to provide competent and reliable information regarding the subject matter covered. However, the views expressed in this publication are those of the author alone, and should not be taken as expert instruction or professional advice. The reader is responsible for his or her own actions.

The author hereby disclaims any responsibility or liability whatsoever that is incurred from the use or application of the contents of this publication by the

Table of Contents

Introduction

Knitting in the round, often known as circular knitting, can seem intimidating at first. I recall seeing someone knitting with four needles for the first time. I was terrified; the item resembled a pincushion! I assumed I'd never be able to replicate same and that there was no use in learning it. Today, I don't think twice about picking up four or five needles, casting on, and knitting in the round endlessly.

Knitting in the round, often known as circular knitting, produces a seamless tube such as in socks, sweaters, and hats. When you work in the round, you'd first cast on a number of stitches, then join the first and last cast-on stitches to continue knitting; the knitting spirally progresses in rounds (like the rows in flat knitting).

Circular knitting has numerous benefits. The fabric's weight is uniformly distributed on the needles, reducing stress on the arms and wrists. Purling is not necessary in stockinette stitch, which is frequently seen as one of the huge benefits of circular knitting. The creation of garments like sweaters is also made easier because knitting in the round nearly completely removes the finishing processes of sewing the sweater together.

There are various techniques, tips, tools, and troubleshooting tricks you must be familiar with, which are all covered in this book and vital for your success in circular knitting. This book aims to provide you with virtually all that you need to be a master in circular knitting; although having prior experience in knitting is an important requirement to get the ball rolling right off the bat.

Without further ado, let's get started.

Chapter 1

Circular Knitting Basics

What is Circular Knitting?

Circular knitting, sometimes known as knitting in the round, is a technique for creating a seamless tube (winds around in a helix to produce the tube).

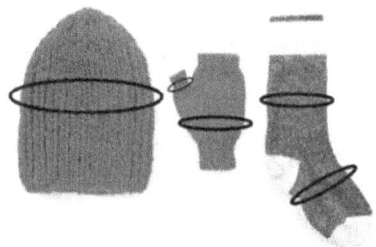

The above incorporates the shape of a tube

Knitting in the round begins by casting on stitches in the same way that flat knitting is started but then connecting the ends of that stitch's row to make a circle. It's most commonly used to create accessories like hats, gloves, and socks, but it could also be used in knitting a sweater's body or sleeves. When knitting in the round, you'll need at least one circular knitting needle or a pair of double-pointed needles (DPNs).

Circular knitting has been more prevalent in recent years as a result of the potential to produce knitting projects with less sewn seams, with some knitters preferring not to knit flat on straight needles entirely. For instance, knitters can create variants on a rectangular or triangular shape when knitting flat on straight needles. This implies that, for example, sweaters must be knit in parts, with different front and back panels as well as two flat sleeves that must be seamed. On the other hand, some knitters despise the task of seaming clothes together after they've finished knitting. Because the body of a sweater can be knit in one unit, with divisions between front and back produced at the armholes, circular knitting thereby removes the necessity for most seams. Instead of being sewn, you can knit sleeves as tubes and have them grafted onto a sweater's body.

Knitting machines can also do circular knitting: you can assemble a double-bed machine to knit in one direction on the front bed and on the back bed in the reverse direction, forming the tube.

Pros and Cons of Circular Knitting

Pros

Minimal Seaming

Another advantage of circular knitting is not having to "seam" that much seaming if any at all. For instance, consider mittens or socks: if either of these is worked as tubes with a few heel or thumb shaping, you will have a negligible seaming. Like hats, mittens, socks, and sweaters, several garments are far more enjoyable when made with no seams. Seams can be rigid and thick, which makes garments unpleasant in areas with high friction levels, such as the armpits or end of sleeves. If a sweater's sleeves are knitted in the round, there is no need to have them seamed after you have finished knitting. If the sweater's body is knitted circularly, you could simply join the sleeves whilst you knit the sweater rather than sewing the sleeves in thereafter. The rationale is that when parts of the sweaters are knitted as tubes, the necessity to seam can be avoided, thus speeding up the knitting process and producing a more pleasant and wearable garment.

The Right Side Faces You Always

Knitting in the round mostly indicates that the right side of your project faces you. Knitting in the round might make tracking your pattern much easier when you work with stranded colorwork. When you work with the pattern in front of you, it makes it easier to maintain the various colors where they belong. This applies to craft with patterns like cables and lace. The route of a pattern chart is simple to grasp and adhere to when the right side faces you constantly, thereby implying lesser mistakes.

Simplicity in Assessing Fitting

Circular knitting allows you to test garments on the go and make alterations as required. When a sleeve is being knitted circularly, for example, it's simple to put it on and assess the length. On the other hand, if you're working flat, you'd need to pin or sew the sleeve with each other for the time being before you try it on. When you work a hat circularly, it enables you to test it out and evaluate the fitting of both the brim's circumference and the hat's depth. Testing the piece facilitates a better fit compared to when you measure and wonder when to stop.

The Gauge is Constant

Some persons knit and purl at various tensions or purl with a little more yarn. For this reason, when a piece is worked flat, they tend to have an irregular gauge. Rowing out is a term used to describe this situation.

This seems like a shorter row of knit stitches that alternates with a somewhat longer row of stitches while working in stockinette stitch. Circular knitting addresses this issue by enabling you to work on the exterior of the piece at all times.

Provides Some Level of Comfortability

When a huge project is knitted on one-pointed needles, it can put a lot of pressure on your wrists, elbows, and hands because the piece's weight drapes from the far edges of your straight needles. On the other hand, this isn't much of an issue when knitting in the round because the piece drapes from the cord, distributing the weight more evenly; the piece's weight drops directly onto your lap while knitting.

Minimal Purling

Purling is disliked by certain knitters. Purling can be somewhat slower compared to knitting, based on your knitting style. Knitting in the round is for you if you prefer stockinette knitting over purling. When knitting in stockinette, you can knit as much as you can since you will be working in a helix manner around the exterior of the item. Knitting a stockinette item in the round can be pretty calming!

Cons

Horizontal Stripes Comes with Some Jogs

Horizontal stripes and colorwork patterns are worked back and forth in rows when you knit flat. These stripes can be matched up pretty identically on every side when the piece is later seamed so that every stripe would seem like a complete circle. It is a painstaking process, but this can be accomplished.

You're actually creating spirals when horizontal stripes or colorwork patterns are worked circularly. This implies that the last stitch knitted at the round's end would seem as though it is elevated above that round's first stitch. When colors are changed, this will form a small stairstep known as a "color jog."

The noticeable change in color and the necessity to painstakingly match colors in seams post-knitting are both eliminated with a "jogless" jog, which is discussed in chapter 2.

Without Seams, Yarn Ends Cannot Be Concealed

Seams in flat knitting provide a spot to conceal yarn ends when colors are changed or when a fresh yarn ball is added. Because knitting in the round has no seams, there is "no spot to conceal." This implies that you'll have to be a little neater while your ends are weaved in. Nevertheless, I consider this a bonus; in flat knitting, the seams can soon get clogged with yarn ends, creating bulk.

Tools and Accessories

Needles for Circular Knitting

Knitting in the round uses both double-pointed and circular needles. Even though some needles are better for certain projects, your choice of needle is primarily a case of what your preference is. The following guidelines will assist you in making an informed choice when purchasing circular knitting needles.

Fixed Circular Needle

Circular needles come in a fixed form and are made up of two-needle tips joined together by a tiny cable or cord. These circular needles are often used in knitting pieces whose circumference is about 18-inches or more. Nevertheless, they can also be used in inventive ways in knitting smaller circumferences.

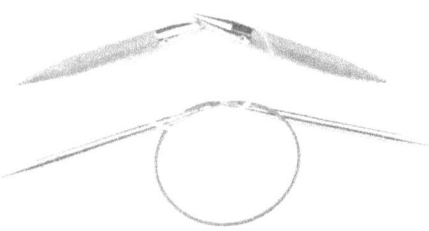

Fixed circular needles come in regular sizes. They are, unfortunately, difficult to come by in sizes lower than US 0 or higher than US 19. Fixed circular needles are available in various cord lengths that range from 9 to 60 inches. The needle's length (not only the cord or cable's length) is also included in this measurement.

The needle tip's length changes with the complete circular needle's length.

Tip: The part of the circular needle where the needle and the cord or cable connect is called the join. It's crucial to have a clean join so your stitches don't "grab" while sliding them to the needles from the cable.

Head Sizes and Cord Lengths

You may have assumed that larger circular needles make nicer stitches, but you are very wrong! Each circular needle size (head size) and cord length has a specific use. A number is assigned to each needle size, and the lower the number, the smaller the circular needle, which will also require that you use a thinner yarn.

When you're working on a pattern, the ideal needle size for knitting in the round will most likely be specified in the description of the pattern. For example, a circular knitting needle with a needle head size of 9 inches and a length of 24 inches is referred to as a 9 24-inch size needle.

The needle's head sizes are usually available in metric or US sizes. Since a 10mm and a US 10 size needle aren't the same, you must ensure to know the sizing convention of your needle.

Needles can also be gotten in UK sizes, which have the reverse sizing convention as the US - the smaller the number, the larger the needle. However, we shall use the US sizing system throughout our discussions of circular needle head sizes.

We'll go through the various circular needle head sizes and cord lengths, as well as their usage; this will assist you in choosing the right circular knitting needle for your project.

Head Sizes

Sizes 1 and Below

These are commonly used for lace and other projects that take a lot of patience. These small needles are difficult to come by and are usually customized. Knitters who are just starting out can overlook these needle sizes.

Sizes 1-3

These range of needle sizes is excellent for those that are obsessed with knitting comfy socks. Most socks are knitted using size 1 and 2 needles with sock yarn, but you may come across patterns that are heavier and utilize non-sock yarns. With these needles and sock yarns, shawls can likewise be knitted in addition to socks.

Sizes 3-5

Size 3-5 needles are used for sport-weight yarns that are a little thicker than sock yarns. These needles can be used in knitting socks, baby blankets, sweaters, and other pieces with sport-weight yarns.

Sizes 5-7

DK-weight yarns are a little lighter than worsted-weight yarns; thus, these sizes of needles are ideal for them. They are mostly used to knit gloves, sweaters, and scarves.

Sizes 7-9

The needle sizes are perhaps the most common, and they're best for knitting worsted-weight yarns. For beginner knitters, these are a good choice.

Sizes 9-11

You'll be able to knit faster as the size of the head increases. The most popular yarns for fast knits are chunky-weight or bulky yarns. For bulky yarns, almost any knitting needle type can be used; however, circular needles are excellent for knitting big projects.

Sizes 11-17

If you want to work on larger projects with bulky yarns, go for this. However, don't be startled if you can't see needle sizes of 12, 14, and 16, as these are only offered in odd sizes (11,13,15, and 17).

Needle Sizes Bigger than 17

Jumbo weight yarns require needle heads that are bigger than size 17 to create exceptionally thick knits. Since they contribute to the weight of the yarns, metal, and wood circular needles are unsuitable for thick knits. It is suggested that you go for plastic knitting needles.

Cord Lengths

9-Inch Cord Length

These are ideal for socks, baby hats, narrow sleeves and other small-circumference projects. These are the shortest needles available in the marketplace. Because the cord is so short, the needles must be short as well. DPNs would be great for projects that require a considerable small circumference since knitting such projects with circular needles can be highly unpleasant owing to the head size of the needle.

16-Inch Cord Length

These cords are great for projects slightly larger for DPNs, especially when knitting circularly. Below are some examples of projects you could accomplish using this length of cord:

- Hats for grown-ups and kids
- Baby sweaters and booties
- Adult sweater's sleeves and collars
- Brims of hats

24-Inch Cord Length

Nearly every single project, particularly sweaters, can be worked on using 24" circular needles. Keep to small shawls, small adult pullovers knitted in the round, and children's pullovers and cardigans if you desire extra room on the needles when you knit.

29-32 Inch Cord Length

Cord lengths of 29 inches are great to use when you need to knit medium-sized pieces in circular or flat knits. These lengths are best to begin with if you're using a design that starts with cast-on stitches of 340. They're an excellent fit for the body of round-knit baby cardigans or blankets and pullovers, shawls, and sweaters.

36-40 Inch Cord Length

These are suitable for small circumference projects knitted with the magic loop. When you knit heavier projects with these, you will be very relaxed since all the weight will be transferred to the cord of the needle, allowing for quicker knitting. They're also appropriate for bigger shawls, cardigans, and round-knit pullovers (such as pullovers for men).

Over 40 Inch Cord Length

Long needles are not needed for these lengths of cord, except if you have really big projects (like bed-size blankets) you want to knit in the round or knit sleeves and socks two at a go.

Interchangeable Circular Needle

Circular needles also come in interchangeable forms, which have the same sizes as fixed circular needles. In contrast to fixed circular needles, the parts must be screwed together before the interchangeables are locked in place.

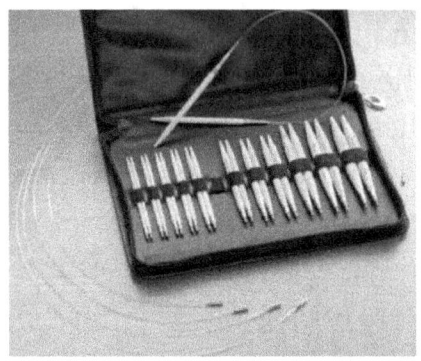

They are often offered as sets, but they are also available in pairs. If you're a knitter with a lot of work-in-progress and unfinished objects, you must know how frustrating it is to run out of needles. To solve this problem, I have copies of my most commonly used sizes in my knitting kits.

Interchangeables are often favored over fixed circulars. Why? I'm grateful you inquired.

1. The cord length can be adjusted (reduced or increased).
2. You can adjust the needle's tip size.
3. Ability to change needle sizes (head size).
4. They are handy in cases of safety, quick accessibility, and mobility.
5. Good for circular and flat knitting.
6. You can knit numerous project sizes.

7. Your work can be locked in place if your knitting needles need to be used for some other project.
8. They're ideal for big projects since they uniformly spread the weight.
9. Cables that are clog-free and/ or spin are available from some brands.

Brands of Circular Knitting Needles

Because metallic and glossy wood needles are sleek and smooth, stitches move quicker along them. Bamboo, unpolished, and plastic wood needles come with more roughness and drag than polished wood needles, which helps keep your stitches in place. These might be a better option to start with.

Circular needles are quite multipurpose and can be used for a variety of tasks.

Below are a few needle choices to consider.

1. While Skacel Addi circulars are more expensive, they provide great value for your money. The Addi circular needles have a flexible cable and an almost invisible join. They come in three categories: Addi Natura, Addi Lace, and Addi Turbo. Addi Natura needles are good starter needles because they are constructed of bamboo

and have a reasonably dull needle tip. Addi Turbos are constructed from nickel-plated brass, making them extremely smooth and quick to use. Addi Lace needles are constructed from polished brass with a pointed tip, making them ideal for lace and cable projects.

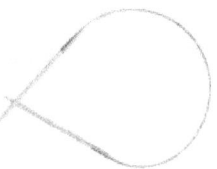

2. Circular needles from Inox are classified into two categories: Inox and Inox Express. Both are reasonably priced. Inox's needle tips are made of coated gray aluminum with a transparent plastic cable. Because the needle's covering produces some friction, it's a good choice to learn knitting in the round. The cable, on the other hand, is not so flexible. The needle tips on Inox Express are nickel-plated, featuring a black cable with flexibility and a clean join.

3. Clover Takumi bamboo needles are reasonably priced and, thanks to their bamboo construction, are ideal for a beginner circular knitter. Nevertheless, in certain cases, your work can get trapped by their "join."

There are several other circular needles out there, but the above-mentioned are perfect for getting started with. Testing out various circular needle types is the ideal route to figure out what performs better for you. This does not have to be a significant upfront investment. Purchase a set at a time and test them for some time before you add another set of separate sizes and lengths. With time, you'll amass a collection of needles that are appropriate for various scenarios and projects; you'll also figure out which ones you mostly prefer to work with.

Double Pointed Needles

Double-pointed needles (DPNs) are straight needles with pointy tips on both endpoints (in contrast to the regular flat needles with just one endpoint). They're ideal to use when you need to work on small-circumference projects that may not be suitable for fixed and interchangeable circular needles. DPNs can be used to make projects like the fingers of your gloves, hats, socks, garments for children, and mittens. With DPNs, you will need to distribute your stitches amongst the needles (which come in four or five sets) and work in a continual helix from one needle to the next to form a knitted tube of fabric. I suggest you start with a set of five needles because, if you are like me, that is infamous for losing needles, the last and fifth needle will serve as a backup plan if one needle is lost, leaving you with the remaining four to work with.

DPNs come in regular sizes, from small 8/0 to the really big US 36 (20mm). DPNs are also available in lengths that range anywhere from 4 – 16 inches, with the most popular lengths being 5 - 8 inches.

Bamboo, steel, plastic, and other wood types are among the materials used in making DPNs.

WOOD   PLASTIC   BAMBOO   STEEL

If you are a beginner, then start with bamboo (especially Clover bamboo) or wooden needles. Surface grip and drag are excellent in both materials, which will make your yarn less slippery on the needle. You may choose steel or aluminum needles as you gain experience with circular knitting because of their smooth nature and speed.

Yarn

There are several varieties of yarn and can be found in several textures, thicknesses (known as yarn weight), and materials, so choose wisely!

Beginner knitters should start with worsted weight yarn because it is less expensive and the right choice to learn new techniques. If you love wool yarn, which is elastic (thus forgiving of unequal beginner's tension) and durable, you can go for it. This category includes several lovely options, including alpaca. You can also consider going for smooth and light-colored yarns to clearly see your stitches' details which is vital, especially when you want to learn a new technique.

You'll undoubtedly explore various fibers as your confidence grows. Indie dyed yarns are incredibly popular, yet they are significantly more expensive than commercial brands. Do not even consider going for novelty yarn, such as bobble yarn, unless you've got enough experience because it's difficult to use.

Other Tools

Tapestry Needles

A tapestry needle (also known as a darning needle) comes with a long, blunt tip used in sewing a knitting piece together and weaving in the ends and tails of yarn; this needle is not to be confused with sharp-pointed sewing needles.

Tapestry needle is also ideal when you want to seam or finish certain techniques such as the kitchener and mattress stitch.

Tapestry needle exists in two types: straight and curved tips. Some knitters like using a sharp endpoint in weaving ends in as they move through the threads.

Although plastic tapestry needles are available, steel tapestry needles are more sturdy and last longer. Ensure the needle's eye is sufficiently large to fit through your fiber, especially if you will be working with bulky fiber.

Scissors

These will come in handy for cutting yarn threads and fixing mistakes from knitted items. Sharp scissors are recommended to avoid unintentional snags or tears in your knitting pattern.

Because material snips are somewhat large, embroidery scissors are a perfect option. However, if you knit frequently, you should invest in a smaller set of snips that you can carry around with you.

Stitch Holders

Stitch holders are similar to huge safety pins. When a pattern instructs you to cast aside certain stitches to return to afterward (more like to keep your work in progress from dropping off while you work on another knitting project piece), you'd simply have them slipped onto the stitch holder.

Stitch Markers

Stitch markers are small rings that are slipped onto your knitting needles to keep track of certain positions in your knitting pattern. For instance, marking the start of a row when knitting circularly (in the round) or when there is a repetition.

A dropped stitch, which indicates the beginning of a fresh knitting round, is also held by stitch markers. The wrong or right side of your knitted garment is shown by a stitch marker, and the number of stitches on the needle is tracked.

For newbies and advanced knitters who prefer not losing their position in a sophisticated design, stitch markers are a must-have knitting tool.

Measuring Tape

This is used in measuring a knitted item or garment and in knitting swatches. It is also useful to have one handy in case you need to measure something else!

Needle Gauge

Because few of us move with a tape measure, needle gauges are ideal for traveling. These gauges are great for determining the sizes of unlabeled knitting needles (by sliding your unlabeled needle into the various holes until you get a matching size). A ruler accompanies some needle gauges to help measure your knitted swatch (confirmation of your gauge) by checking the number of stitches knitted per inch/centimeter, typically across a 4" or 10cm measurement. Some needle gauge are square in shape, where you will have to position it over your knitted swatch to take your measurement, as shown below.

Crochet Hook

Even if you don't know how to crochet, it's good to have one crochet hook at a minimum. A size E (US 3.5mm) crochet hook is an excellent all-around tool. It can be used to correct mistakes like dropped stitches or to pick up stitches along your work's edges.

Row Counters

Certain patterns call for you to keep count of the number of rows you've knit, and a row counter would help you do this. Several row counters can slide into your needle and feature a number dial that can be changed after each row. Some of them feature a simple button that you press, as shown below. Yes, smartphone apps exist for that as well.

Chapter 2

Getting Started With Circular Knitting

Knitting Terms and Abbreviations

The following contains a list of the prevalent knitting acronyms, terminology, and meanings from modern knitting patterns worldwide.

Knitting Abbreviations A-C

Knitting Abbreviation	Explanation
alt	Alternate/Alternating
approx	Approximately
beg	Beginning
bet	Between
BO	Bind Off (Cast Off)
byo	Backward Yarn Over
C4B	Slip the next 2 stitches onto the cable needle and leave them at the **back**. K2, then K2 from the cable needle
C4F	Slip the next 2 stitches onto the cable needle and leave them at the **front**. K2, then K2 from the cable needle
CA	Colour A
CB	Colour B
CC	Contrasting Colour
cdd	Centred Double Decrease
cl	Cross Left
cm	Centimeter
cn	Cable Needed

CO	Cast On/Cast Off
Cont	Continue
Cross 2 L	Cross 2 stitches to the left
Cross 2 R	Cross 2 stitches to the right

Knitting Abbreviations D-K

Knitting Abbreviation	Explanation
Dec	Decrease. Eliminate one or more stitches. Usually the pattern will tell you exactly how to do this.
DPN	Double Pointed Needles
DTR	Double Treble
EON	End of Needle
EOR	End of Row
FC	Front Cross
FL	Front Loop
Foll	Follow
g	Grams
g st	Garter Stitch
Inc	Increase. Add one or more stitches.
K	Knit Stitch
k1B	Knit into the stitch 1 row below.
K1tbl	Knit the next stitch through the back of the loop
K2tog	Knit two together
K2togtbl	Knit two together through back loops
K3(4)tog	Knit the next 3(4 n) stitches together
kfb	Knit into the front and back of a stitch

36

krl	Knit through right loop.
ksp	Knit 1, then slip back to the left hand needle. Lift the second stitch on the left hand needle back over the original stitch and replace the returned stitch on the righthand needle.
kwise	Knit-wise

Knitting Abbreviations L-M

Knitting Abbreviation	Explanation
LC	Left Cross
LH	Left Hand
LP	Loop
LT	Left Twist
m	Meter
M1	Make 1 stitch
M1K	Make one stitch knitwise (single knit increase)
M1l	Make one left-leaning stitch
M1lp	Make one left-leaning stitch purlwise
M1P	Make one stitch purlwise (single purl increase)
M1R	Make one right-leaning stitch
M1rp	Make one right-leaning stitch purlwise
Maintain	Maintain the center block of the pattern. Add or remove stitches at each end of the center without disturbing the pattern.
MB	Make Bobble
MC	Main colour
mm	Millimeter

Knitting Abbreviations N-P

Knitting Abbreviation	Explanation
No	Number
Oz	Ounce
p	Purl Stitch
p tbl, P1 tbl, or P1b	Purl through the back loop
p2sso	Pass 2 slipped stitches over
p2tog	Purl 2 stitches together
p2togtbl	Purl 2 stitches together through back loops
pat or patt	Pattern
pfb	Purl 1 into the front and back of stitch
pm	Place Market
pnso	Pass the next stitch over
prev	Previous
psso	Pass slipped stitches over
pwise	Purlwise

Knitting Abbreviations R-S

Knitting Abbreviation	Explanation
Rem	Remaining
Rep	Repeat
Rev st st	Reverse Stockinette Stitch
RH	Right Hand
Rnd	Round(s)
RS	Right Side
S2KP2	Slip 2 stitches as if to knit them together, knit 1, pass 2 slipped stitches over knit stitch
sk	Skip
sk2p	Slip 1, knit 2 together, pass slipped stitch over (a double decrease)
SKP	Slip 1 knitwise, knit 1, pass slip stitch over knit stitch
sl	Slip
sl st	Slip Stitch
Sl1	Slip next stitch knitwise
Sl1k	Slip 1 Knitwise
Sl1p	Slip 1 Purlwise
sm	Slip Marker
ssk	Slip next 2 stitches knitwise one at a time, then knit them through back loops together
ssp	Slip, Slip, Purl
SSPP2	Slip 2 stitches knitwise then slip them as if to p2tog through back loops. Purl 1, pass 2 slipped stitches over purl stitch

39

sssk	Slip 3 stitches knitwise, knit these 3 stitches together through back loops
sssp	Slip 3 stitches knitwise, return these 3 stitches to left needle and purl these 3 stitches together through back loops
st	Stitch
st st	Stockinette Stitch

Knitting Abbreviations T-Y

Knitting Abbreviation	Explanation
tbl	Through back loop
tfl	Through front loop
tog	Together
w&t	Wrap and Turn
Work Even	Continue with no increases or decreases.
WS	Wrong Side
wyib	With yarn in back
wyif	With yarn in front
yb	Yarn Back
yd	Yard
yf	Yarn Front
yfwd or yf	Yarn Forward
yo	Yarn Over
yo2	Yarn Over Twice
yon	Yarn Over Needle
yrn	Yarn Round Needle

Terms & Common Measurements

Term	Description
*	repeat the instructions following the single asterisk as directed
* *	repeat instructions between asterisks as many times as directed or repeat at specified locations
{ }	work instructions within brackets as many times as directed
[ ]	work instructions within brackets as many times as directed
( )	work instructions within parentheses as many times as directed or work a group of stitches all in the same stitch or space

Measurement	Description
" or in	inch
cm	centimeter
g	gram
m	meter
mm	millimeter
oz	ounce
yd	yard

Knitting Chart Symbols

Stitch charts have replaced written guidelines in several knitting patterns. In most cases, these charts use the conventional set of symbols vetted by the Craft Yarn Council.

When you knit a pattern that calls for a particular symbol, regularly examine the pattern key to ensure that the standard definitions are consistent. Every symbol, in most cases, symbolizes a stitch as it appears on the work's right side.

Right-slanting make 1

Left-slanting make 1

Right-slanting lifted inc

Left-slanting lifted inc

Sl 1 purlwise wyb on RS, sl 1 purlwise wyf on WS

Sl 1 purlwise wyf on RS, sl 1 purlwise wyb on WS

K3tog on RS, p3tog on WS

P3tog on RS, k3tog on WS

SK2P on RS, SSSK on RS, SSSP on WS

SSSP on RS, SSSK on WS

S2KP2 on RS, SSPP2 on WS

K1 tbl on RS, p1 tbl on WS

P1 tbl on RS, k1 tbl on WS

Bobble

Sts do not exist in these areas of chart

Inc 1-to-3

Inc 1-to-4

Inc 1-to-5

Dec 4-to-1 (right slanting)

Dec 4-to-1 (left slanting)

Dec 4-to-1 (centered)

Dec 5-to-1

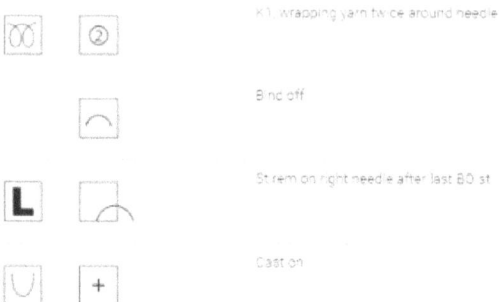

K1, wrapping yarn twice around needle

Bind off

St rem on right needle after last BO st

Cast on

Knitting Gauge

One of the essential preparations before you knit a project is to knit a gauge swatch. In its most basic form, a knitting gauge swatch is a little preview of the expected finished piece. It's typically a knitted square produced with the yarn, pattern, and needles you'll be using for your project.

If you will be knitting a piece with a specific size, ensure you knit a swatch first.

I understand...

The universal groan is audible. But, if you will spend time knitting a sweater or another fitted garment, won't it be lovely if it fits?

Let's be honest here. You have put lots of effort and money into your craft. Why make a half-assed attempt at a knitting pattern without first knitting a gauge swatch? There's no reason not to, and it will help you become a better knitter. There. I've made my point.

A number of other reasons exist that call for swatching. To begin, a knitted swatch is used to establish a knitting gauge. For this to happen, you'd have to take a look at how your yarn, knitting needles, and knitting tension interplay. Swatching is the only approach to adequately assess this.

Swatching will reveal whether or not:

- Your needles are suitable for the intended project
- The yarn you intend using is suitable for the intended project
- You need to acquire or develop more expertise in a particular skill
- You need to adjust the tension of your knitting
- You need to gain enough experience in blocking
- The project or pattern deserves to be completed

To conclude, it's essential to swatch before you knit to ascertain if your tools will collaborate well enough.

What exactly does this imply?

Sadly, not all yarn and needles are compatible. Furthermore, not all yarn materials are of the same size and feel. You'll need the appropriate tools and supplies to make a knitted piece that won't be dumped, such as yarn and knitting needles.

Knitting a swatch will help you decide whether the yarn and tools are valuable to you or whether you should look for alternatives. All of this is required to meet the knitting gauge.

Now, let's delve a little deeper into knitting gauge

What is Knitting Gauge?

The number of rows for every vertical inch and the number of stitches for every horizontal inch is known as the knitting gauge. It's crucial to understand this since the size of your completed piece is determined by these measurements.

When you read a knitting pattern, look for the brand of knitting needle and its size, as well as the yarn used in making the project, which a designer will specify in most of their projects.

Assuming the knitting pattern calls for worsted-weight Cascade 220 yarn. The tools and supplies the designer lists for the gauge can be a size 8 (10mm) knitting needle and the swatch knitted in stockinette stitch.

The pattern also should incorporate a specific gauge.

Below is how the gauge will look:

20 stitches/28 rows = 4" in stockinette stitch

This implies 20 stitches (in width) and 28 rows (in height) gauge totaling a square of four inches in stockinette stitch. The aim is to align with the designer's stitch and row gauge listed on the pattern.

Per this information, a pattern swatch should be knitted with the same yarn (or a comparable worsted weight yarn) and a knitting needle of size 8.

Knitting Swatch In The Round

Working your swatch as you intend working the finished project is the secret to determining your gauge accurately. If a sweater is knitted in the round, your swatch should also be knitted in the round.

It is common knowledge among regular knitters that purling is done on the wrong side when you knit stockinette flat; for several knitters, however, the purl stitches are a bit freer than the knit stitches. However, when stockinette is knit in the round, knit stitches are only worked. As a result, if your sweater is knitted in the round with all knit stitches, you'd have to replicate same with your swatch.

This does not apply to just a stockinette scenario; it's standard practice to have your swatch knitted as you would with your sweater.

Knitting a swatch in the round does not have to be stressful, thanks to the speed-swatching method explained below, which lets you knit a bigger swatch with a convenient workaround.

So, take up your circular needle of any size as we demonstrate how to knit a speed swatch.

Step 1

Cast on like you normally do. Ensure that your swatch has a height and width of 4-6 inches, at a minimum. The measurement will read more accurately if your swatch is made bigger.

The cast-on stitches should be slipped across the needle's opposite end. At this point, you should have the working yarn close to the circular needle's cord.

Step 2

Knit onto the empty needle while the working yarn is held gently around the back.

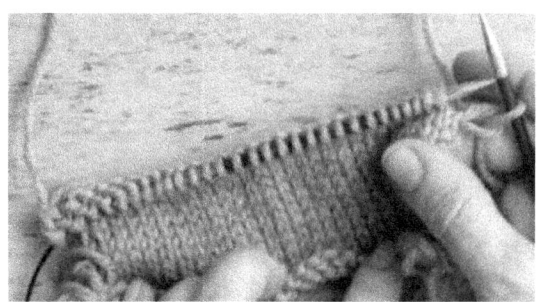

Work all the way through.

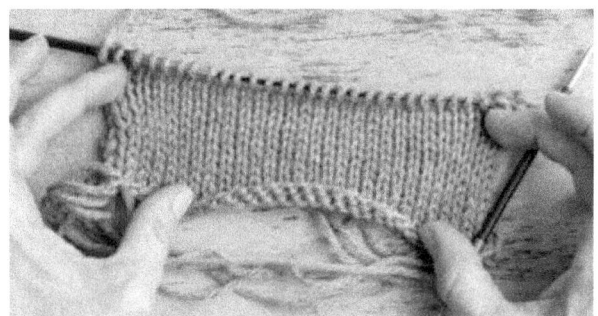

Step 3

The stitches should be slipped back to the other needle on getting to the row's end. Knit across the row anew, and remember to leave the working yarn free throughout the back of your work.

Step 4

Repeat steps 2 and 3 until your swatch is complete. Then bind off as you normally do.

Below is how your swatch will look from behind:

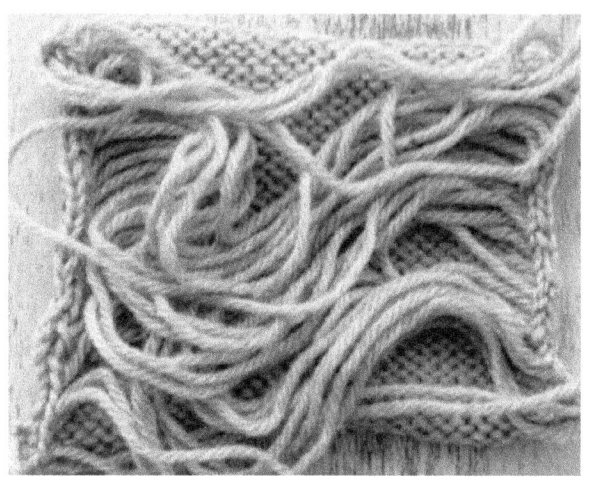

Clip the yarn floating from behind if they're very tight and pull on your knitting, just like the blue swatch here. They wouldn't come apart, and your swatch reading will be more precise when measured.

If you suspect your gauge is off while knitting, swap to another needle midway through, just like the swatch above, such that one swatch can then be washed and dried, making it easy to compare the gauges.

Remember to have your swatch blocked if you wish to block your completed project.

Measuring Your Gauge Swatch

A gauge includes stitches and rows.

Get a ruler, a measuring tape, or a needle gauge (one that can also measure a swatch).

Insert a pin in the stitch beside the edge of your swatch to determine your stitch gauge. Next, take a measurement of 10cm/4″ from where you inserted your pin, then insert another pin. Ensure you keep to the line of horizontal stitches. Count the stitches (the sequence of "Vs" beside each other) among the two pins, noting it somewhere or committing it to memory.

Repeat the same vertically to get the measurement of the row gauge.

Don't overlook half stitches and rows within the 10cm/4" section - partial stitches and rows need to be accounted for. They add a substantial measurement to the overall project.

So what if you have your gauge wrongly measured?

Let us assume you wanted to get 9 stitches for every inch but only got 6 stitches per inch. This suggests your stitches are a little freer than what your pattern called for; in such a case, you have to knit a second swatch with a smaller needle to firm them up. Take your measurement again after binding off.

If you're having the reverse issue, such as shooting for 9 stitches per inch but getting 13 rather, your needle size would need to move up by 1 to loosen up your knitting.

Continue swatching and altering needle sizes until you achieve the desired gauge. You'll knit the overall project with the winning needles.

If switching needle sizes does not help, or if you have a really off gauge, it's possible that your chosen yarn isn't the proper fit for the project. If you still desire to use that yarn, simply adjust the pattern. Go over everything carefully to see how many multiples you'd have to subtract or add. If your pattern's body is a five-stitch repeat, for instance, add or remove five stitches.

Knitting Jogless Stripes In The Round

Anyone who enjoys knit stripes in the round will be acquainted with the dreadful jog. A jog is that small downhill drop in your knitting where you switch the color at the start of the round. It spoils the completed project's sleek, flawless look, creating unending pain for stripe enthusiasts.

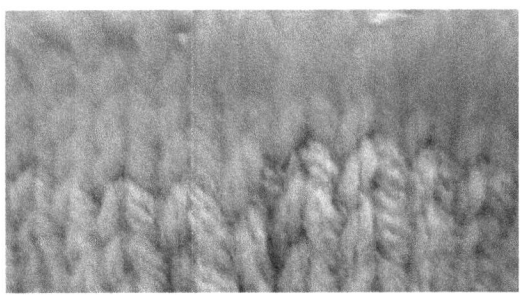

Understanding the reason for this jog is the starting point toward resolving it. When knitting in the round, we are not merely stacking a circle of knitting over another; instead, we're knitting in a constant spiral. As a result, when a new round is started using a new color, it won't line up beside the previous round's last stitch, but instead, it will sit slightly below it. A few possibilities to reduce the possibility of a jog while knitting in the round are discussed subsequently.

Knit together the first of the two preceding rounds

This is the technique I prefer when I want to avoid the jogless stripe. An experienced knitter could still detect that a fresh round was started there even if they squint due to the extended stitch covering two rounds, but the novice will have no idea. The best aspect of this is that this technique is quite simple; recalling to do it is the most difficult aspect. Here's how to apply this technique.

1. When you are through with your first color of yarn (A) and prepared to begin knitting the second stripe with your opposing color (B), proceed to knit that round, as usual, using your new color.

2. Upon reaching the first stitch of the subsequent round, locate the stitch in color A right beneath the first stitch in color B.

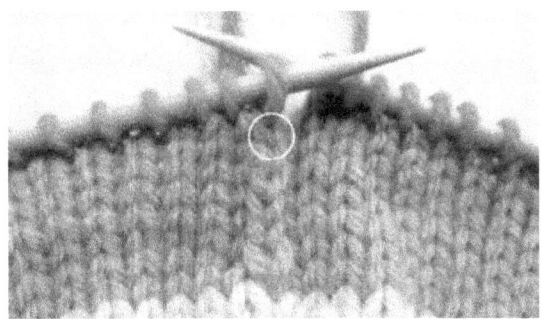

3. Pull up this stitch by the right leg with your right-hand side needle, slipping it onto your left-hand side needle.

4. For the initial stitch of your subsequent round, the stitch should be knit in color A alongside the next stitch close to it (color B's first stitch)

5. Knit all over in color B till you are prepared to change to color A, then repeat the process.

Slip the first round's first stitch

This technique is more thoughtless than the first. To follow this technique, you'd have to knit the stripes as you normally would, but the first stitch is slipped purlwise upon getting to the second round's first stitch in the new color.

Below are the detailed instructions.

1. Knit your first round as you normally would once you are prepared to begin knitting the subsequent stripe with color B.

2. Instead of knitting it, slip the first stitch purlwise upon reaching the subsequent round's first stitch.

3. Knit in color B till you are prepared to change back to color A; repeat the cycle.

Knitting the two colors together

This technique is not frequently discussed where a new round of color is started when you knit with the two colors, then returning to manipulate the beginning of the round upon completion, such that the two colors appear in the first stitch. If you don't want an extended stitch at the start of your round, this is a better substitute for both techniques discussed above.

1. The first stitch should be knit with the two colors (A and B) at the start of the round, where you'll switch to color B.

2. Keep knitting with only the new color for as much as you desire or until you can visibly see the stitches below.

3. Pull at color A yarn end with your needle such that it is on the first stitch of the V's right side with color B on the left side. The first time you try this, it may require a little experimenting to figure out.

Increasing Stitches

When knitting in the round, you can only increase and decrease on the right-hand side of your project. Aside from that, every increase or decrease technique that flat knitting uses is applicable in circular knitting.

Increases make it possible to increase the amount of stitches in a row or round. Knit pieces, like hats, sweaters, and mittens, profit from this technique. Increases can be found in practically any knitting project. It's important to be acquainted with the most popular types of knitting increases so you will be prepared when they appear in a knitting design, some of which are discussed below.

Knitting Front and Back (KFB)

1. **If you do not care about having a bump in your project, you should go for the knit front and back method**. It's simple to increase your stitch when you knit front and back. However, because this increasing technique causes a visible bulge in your knitting, it's not suitable for many projects.

   For instance;

- You can go for the knit front and back increase method when you use a stitch with a texture like the garter stitch.
- KFB is great to use when the "increase" section is concealed, like a sleeve's underside

2. **The subsequent stitch should be knitted without the old one slipping off**. The right-hand needle should be brought in front of the stitch of the left-hand needle.

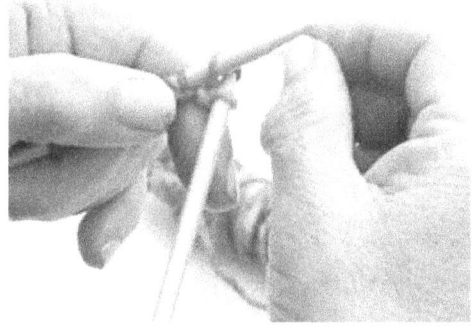

Now, the yarn should be looped across the needle's end.

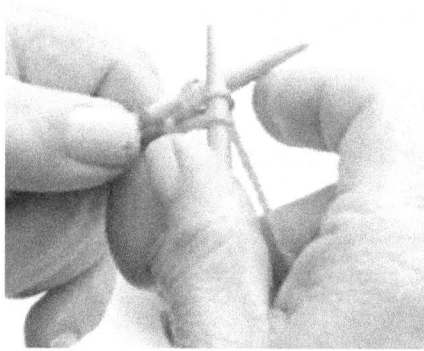

Then, the yarn should be pulled over without allowing the old stitch to drop from the needle just yet.

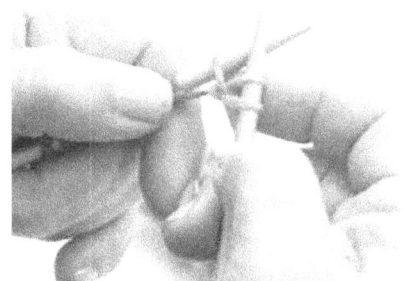

If you intend for this row to be purled, then go
ahead in purling this first stitch without the old
stitch falling off.

3. **Knit with the right-hand needle by inserting it
   behind the same stitch**.

   After the needle is inserted into the stitch, wound
   the yarn around the needle's end, pulling the
   yarn through to end the stitch.

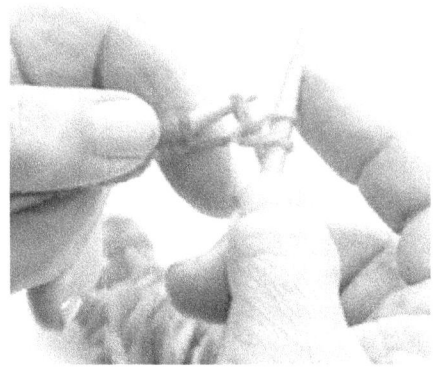

Now, the old stitch should be allowed to drop from the needle's end.

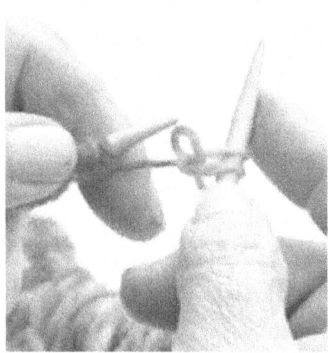 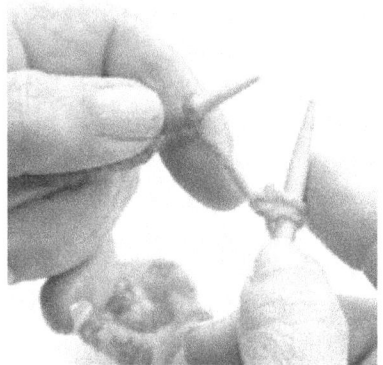

If you intend to purl, then proceed to purl into this stitch.

Making a Stitch (M1)

1. **Put the left-hand needle underneath the yarn between the stitches.** You would see a visible yarn between the two stitches on the needle's right and left-hand. Find this yarn and raise it with the left-hand needle's tip.

You would have to use your fingers to pull the stitches apart to locate the yarn.

2. **Using your fingers, coil the yarn and reattach it to the needle.** Use your index finger and thumb to grab the yarn on the left-hand needle and slide it off the needle. Then coil it again, sliding it onto the needle in its coiled state.

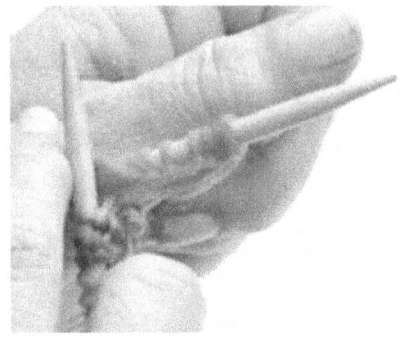

3. **To form a stitch, the new loop should be knit into as you would normally do.** The right-hand needle should be slipped into the coiled loop.

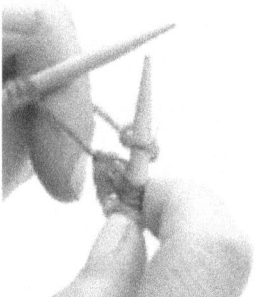 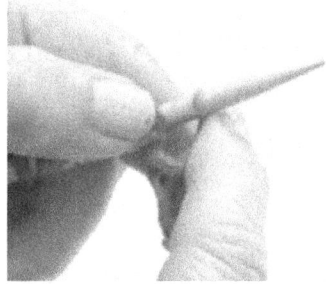

Then yarn over the needle's end.

To make a new stitch, push this loop across the coiled loop.

If you intend for this stitch to be purled, then simply purl into it as you would usually do.

4. **This stitch should likewise be worked in the back if you want to create two.** If you intend to create two stitches from the coiled loop, then

ensure the loop does not slip off your needle upon knitting into it. Instead, knit into the loop's back, then allow the loop to slip off.

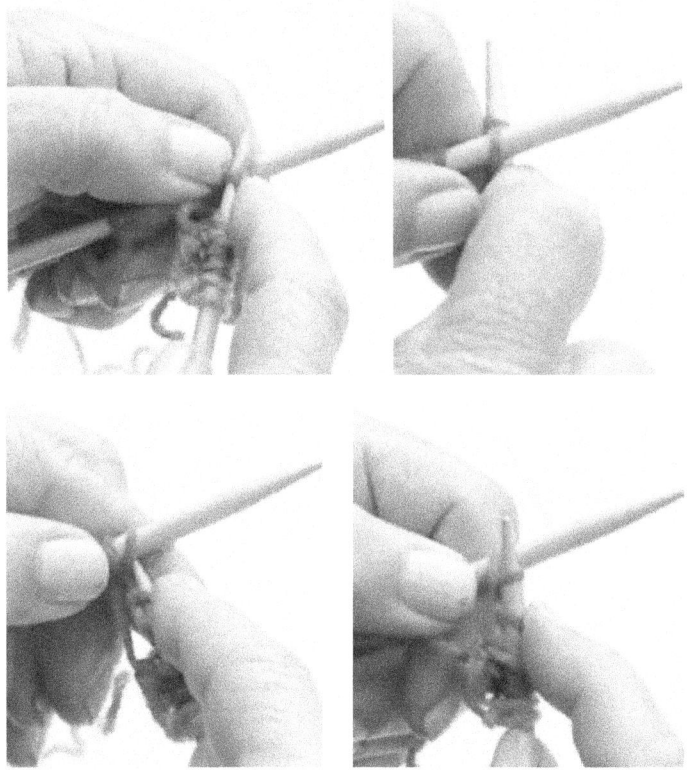

If you want to purl, purl into the stitch's back upon purling into the stitch's front.

Decreasing Stitches

Removing stitches in knitting is very simple, and the easiest method to achieve this is by using the "knit two together" (k2tog) technique. Although many other techniques exist, the k2tog technique is very easy to do, especially for beginners. Remember, if you knit flat, then this method of decreasing stitch should not be new to you because decreasing in flat knitting is just like decreasing in circular knitting.

K2tog entails handling two stitches as though they were one. You will be subtracting a stitch (or loop) from your needle when you k2tog. The consequence is that the number of stitches you have in a row is reduced by a stitch. This changes the shape of the project by reducing its breadth.

Note: Knitting the k2tog with stitches in the center of your piece is recommended. This is because the stitches around your knitting edges might become mushed up and glitchy. However, the instruction below uses the project's first stitch to demonstrate the "knit two together" technique. The instructions are the same whether you do them in the center of your project or at the end.

Instructions

Please notice that I am beginning this instruction with six stitches on my knitting needle's top row. See the image below.

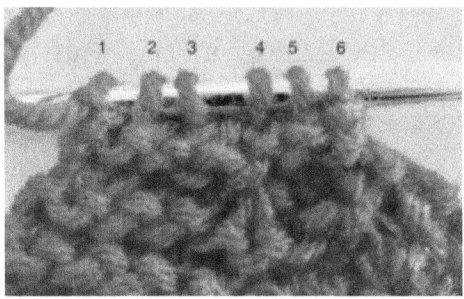

I'm going to reduce those stitches by one.

1. The right-handed needle should be inserted into the first two stitches as if making the knit stitch.

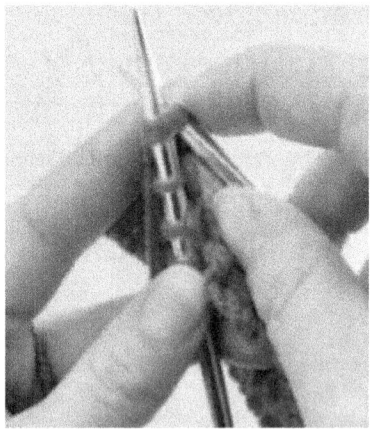

2. As usual, the yarn should be wound around the needle.

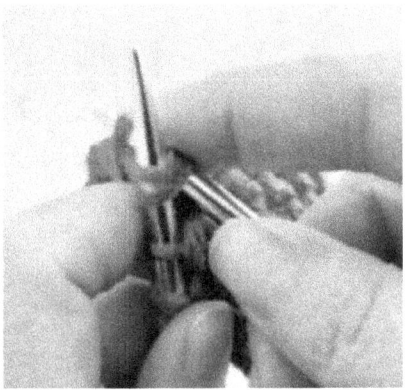

3. The yarn should be pulled across the two stitches, sliding them off the needle simultaneously and allowing them to fall.

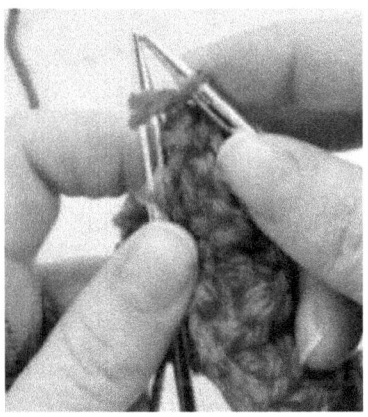

You've finished one knitting decrease.

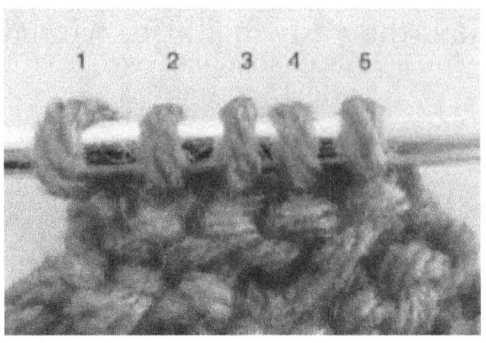

Now, the top row of my knitted project now has just five stitches.

K2tog Important Tips to Remember

Recall how I said earlier that there are many ways to decrease knitting? It's crucial to understand that each form of knitting decrease has its own distinct "look."

When you "knit two together," you get a tight and right-slanted decrease.

This implies you must keep track of whether you're decreasing on a knit or purl stitch to be certain you're using a reduction technique that produces the right stitch to match your pattern or the rest of your project's stitching.

For example, if you're decreasing on a purl stitch rather than a knit stitch, you might want to p2tog ("purl two together"). This results in a slanting decrease to the left.

The p2tog is the same as the k2tog, only you purl rather than knit the two top stitches together.

Chapter 3

Basic Stitches In Circular Knitting

Knit Stitch

Like it or not, this simple stitch is the cornerstone of knitting. The knit stitch is simple to use and produces a gorgeous fabric.

We'd use a slip knot and a long tail cast on (discussed in chapter 5) to start this instruction. Before continuing, double-check that you've completed these steps. You can use your desired circular needle for this activity per the circular knitting needle recommendations provided earlier.

Steps

1. To begin a knit stitch, grab the needle in your left hand with the cast-on row of stitches, then grab the empty needle using your right hand.

2. Slip in your right needle from below to top into the cast-on row's first stitch.

3. Pull the yarn attached to the yarn ball.

4. The yarn should be wound across the needle, from the back to the front.

5. Drag the yarn downward until it emerges through the stitch.

6. Push the needle down slowly and remove the yarn from the needle.

7. The right-hand needle should be inserted into the loop. A brand new stitch is now formed

8. Pull the right-hand needle away from the needle on the left hand.

9. To reinforce the stitch, pull the yarn connected to the yarn ball. Repeat steps 1–9.

Upon knitting the complete row, the yarn connected to the yarn ball will be positioned on the left of your row (i.e., your row's endpoint). The yarn must be on the row's right side to continue knitting (i.e., the row's starting point).

To do this, simply turn the needle around, as shown below;

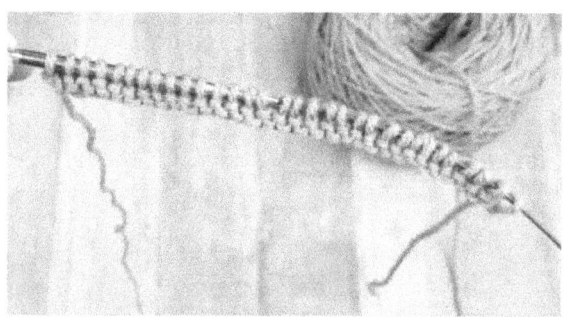

The working yarn (i.e., the yarn attached to the ball of yarn) is now on the row's right side, leaving you with a new row of stitches you can knit with.

Whenever you reach the row's end, simply turn your work around so that the working yarn is facing right. Continue knitting until you reach your desired length.

Purl Stitch

Purling the purl stitch, just like knitting the knit stitch, is a fundamental aspect of knitting.

It may appear to be a difficult stitch; however, this is not the case. Purling is, in reality, the polar opposite of the knit stitch.

You will be able to knit many stitches, including the rib stitch, stockinette stitch, and others, once you have learned how to knit and purl stitches.

Steps

1. Ascertain that the right-hand needle has the working yarn in its front.

2. The needle on the right hand should be slid into the stitch from top to bottom with the working yarn in front.

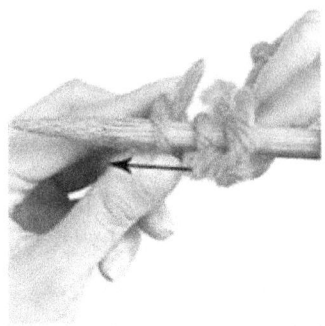

3. The working yarn should be wrapped with the needle on the right hand from the front to the back.

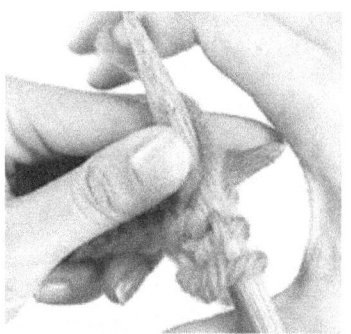

4. Make a loop by wrapping the right needle completely around.

5. Bring the loop beneath and through the left-hand needle's stitch.

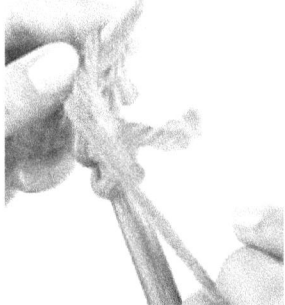

6. The needle on the right hand should be inserted into the loop.

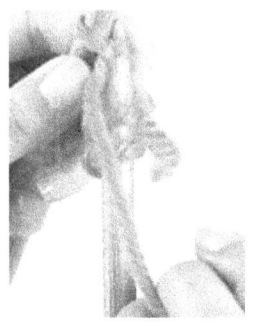

7. Insert the needle completely into the stitch.

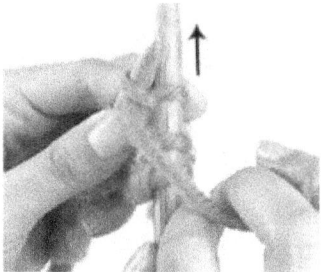

8. The stitch on the left-hand needle should be removed.

The result below is a purl stitch.

Things to Note

Looks are important! A knit resembles a flat V, and a purl resembles a small bump comparable to a pearl seen in an oyster.

Knits   Purls

Knowing how to differentiate a purl stitch from a knit stitch is a terrific skill to have.

Every stitch is two-dimensional; the They have a front and back side

The purl - the small bump – is on the front side of a purl. The purl's back side, on the other hand, may startle you; a purl's back side is a knit stitch - and if this is true, then shrewd readers will conclude that the knit stitch's backside is a purl stitch.

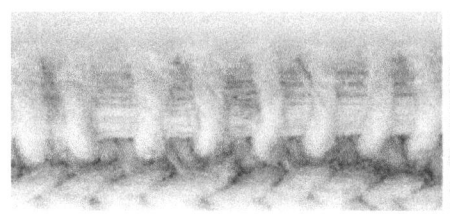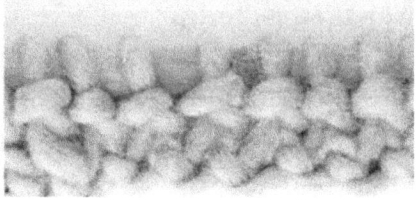

Front Side   Back Side

Garter Stitch

The garter stitch, alongside stockinette stitch, is among the first stitches you'd learn while learning how to knit.

Owing to its thickness and silky texture, garter stitch is ideal for knit scarves and baby blankets. Dishcloths and washcloths are also examples of what you can make with the garter stitch. As a result, regardless of the project you wish to make, you can almost certainly do it with garter stitch.

Garter stitch knitting is the most straightforward stitch to learn if you can make the knit stitch. When knitting flat, it is made up of the knit stitch only.

Garter stitch can be reversed completely, implying that it looks the same on both sides. The finished fabric is extremely elastic in length and in width.

The garter stitch also comprises the knit and purl rows that alternate. You may question if garter stitch isn't merely knit stitches on flat needles. What role do purls play? Remember what I said earlier about a knit stitch's front and back, whereby turning the knit stitch over to the back will give you a purl stitch and vice versa. That is why even if you are not purling any stitches, you will still have the purl stitch emerge in the garter stitch when knitting flat. When you knit stitch, it also results in a purl stitch on the reverse side. You could even conclude that a knit stitch cannot be made without a purl stitch, and vice versa.

Thus, the garter's flat knitting alternating knit/purl arrangement is created by the knit stitch's distinctive two-faced structure.

Although knitting the garter stitch flat means you'd have to use only the knit stitch, this isn't the same when the garter stitch is knit in the round, which demands purling.

How so?

You'd never flip the knitting to the other side when knitting in the round because you will always stay on the knit's side or the front side and will never reach the purl's side, which is the knitting's back. You will wind up with a stockinette stitch rather than a garter stitch if you attempt to knit all the rounds like you would when you knit flat. So you'll have to add your own round of purl for the garter stitch to be knit in the round. Round 2 is for that purpose, which you will see subsequently.

Knitting Garter Stitch in the Round

1. Cast on your desired number of stitches, joining in the round (covered in chapter 5). Ensure the stitches are not twisted.
2. Knit all stitches in the first round.
3. Purl all stitches in the second round
4. Repeat steps 2-3 until your knitting reaches the desired length.

Knowing when to knit and purl

You could be feeling that garter stitch in the round is difficult! How do I keep count of the first and second rounds?

Simple...

Knit the purl stitches and purl the knit stitches whenever you knit the garter stitch in the round.

That should do it.

If you come across a row of knit stitches, simply purl them and if you come across a row of purl stitches, just knit them. Once you recall that garter stitch is simply alternate rows/rounds of knits and purls, this would make logical sense.

Stockinette Stitch

Stockinette stitch is very simple to learn and one of the important stitches you need to learn when knitting just after the garter stitch. Stockinette is the most frequently used stitch found in several patterns; sweaters, caps, mittens, and various knitted items.

Stockinette stitch can be knitted if you can knit and purl.

The stockinette stitch has a "right" and a "wrong" side. The "right" side is intended to be visible. It is composed of knit stitches that resemble small V-shapes facing out.

The fabric that does not face out is the "wrong" side (especially the case when knitting flat), composed of purl stitches.

Because stockinette stitch tends to curl, it's usually enclosed by a flat border.

RIGHT SIDE   WRONG SIDE

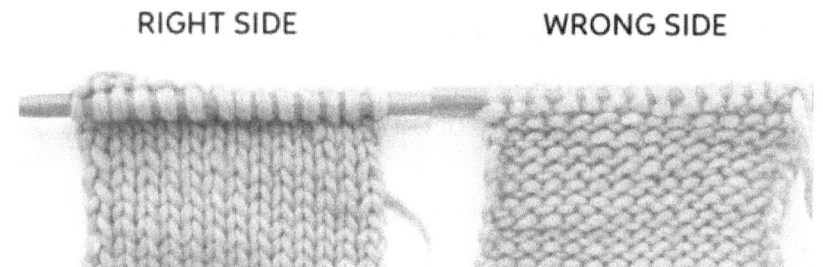

Stockinette stitch in the round

Knitting in the round using stockinette stitch is way easier than knitting flat! Since no "wrong" side exists when knitting in the round, all knitting takes place on the work's "right" side. The stitches that comprise the "right" side of the stockinette stitch are composed only of the knit stitches.

Steps

1. Cast on whatever number of stitches you desire, joining in the round. Ensure the stitches are not twisted.
2. Knit all stitches in round 1 (right side).
3. Repeat round 1 until the item is of your desired length. That's about it!
4. Bind off and weave in your ends as you should with every other stitch you knit

After knitting some rounds, your stockinette stitch will be like the one below

Rib Stitch

You'll undoubtedly need to eventually learn to knit the rib stitch in the round, whether you are knitting socks, hats, or sweaters. Knitting flat ribbing is simple enough for many beginners, but knitting ribbing in the round is a complete story, especially because knitting in the round has no wrong sides.

Ribbing is frequently used in making a pattern's "cuff" while you knit specific items; consider socks and mittens cuffs as examples. This is because ribbing is usually stretchy and somewhat tight compared to other stitches like garter or stockinette stitch. Ribbing will keep your items in place, helping them fit perfectly!

Subsequently, I'll show you how to make the 1x1 and 2x2 rib stitches, which are two of the most used rib stitches.

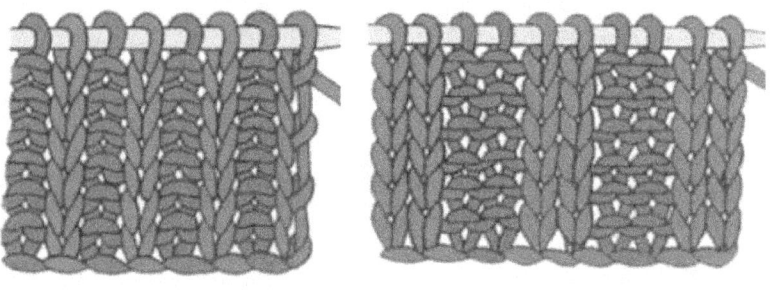

1x1 ribbing   2x2 ribbing

Knits and purls are used in these rib stitches to create a stretchable rib. They are also ideal for novices that are learning to knit and purl.

1×1 Rib Knitting in the Round

1. An even number of cast-on stitches should be made (i.e., 2, 4, 6, 8, 10, and so on)
2. Round 1: *knit 1, purl 1; rep from * to the round's end
    Round 2 plus every other round: the knit stitches should be knitted, and the purl stitches should be purled.
3. Rep rounds 1 and 2 until you achieve your desired length

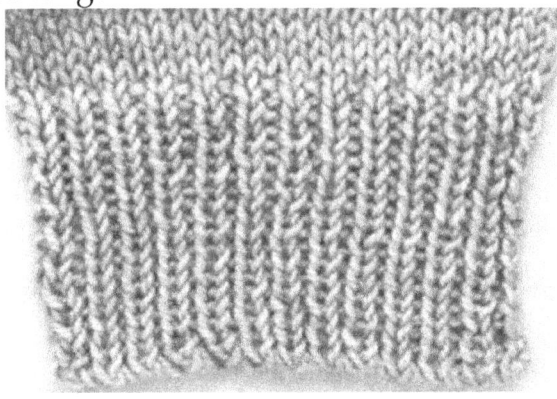

2×2 Rib Knitting in the Round

1. A multiple of 4 cast-on stitches should be made (i.e., 4, 8, 12, 16, 20, and so on)
2. Round 1: *knit 2, purl 2; rep from * to the round's end
    Round 2 plus every other round: the knit stitches

should be knitted, and the purl stitches should be purled.

3. Rep rounds 1 and 2 until you achieve your desired length

Using a pair of smaller needles to knit is the easiest way to obtain a snug and stretchy ribbing. A tighter tension ensures a fabric is both snappy and stretchy.

Horizontal Mattress Stitch

A horizontal mattress stitch is used to connect two stockinette knitted items securely. The mattress stitch is useful in joining your knitting project's cast-on and bind-off edges. This stitch resembles a row of knit stitches, giving the appearance of an "undetectable flawless look." The end effect is quite smooth and tidy.

It's better to utilize the long cast-on yarn tail in seaming the edges up because there will be lesser ends to weave in and lesser knots. At a minimum, the tail needs to be 3x of the length of the edge you'll be seaming (and you'll have to include an additional length to weave the tail in). Use a matching yarn if the tail is not sufficiently long.

Steps

I'd use a contrasting color for demonstrative purposes.

1. With the right sides facing, lay your knitted pieces next to one another and align the edges. You'd have an upper and lower piece. You'll be working from the right side to left.

2. Bottom piece. Find the first stitch, which should be exactly beneath the bind-off edge. Push the yarn using your tapestry needle across the first stitch's middle (from the back to the front via the middle "V").

3. Upper piece. Find the first equivalent stitch right ontop the cast-on. Pull the yarn through by inserting the needle beneath that stitch (underneath the two "V" legs).

4. Bottom piece. The needle should be inserted via the first stitch's middle (i.e., front to back), bringing it up via the subsequent stitch's middle (i.e., back to front)

5. Upper piece. Pull the yarn across by inserting the
   needle beneath the appropriate stitch.

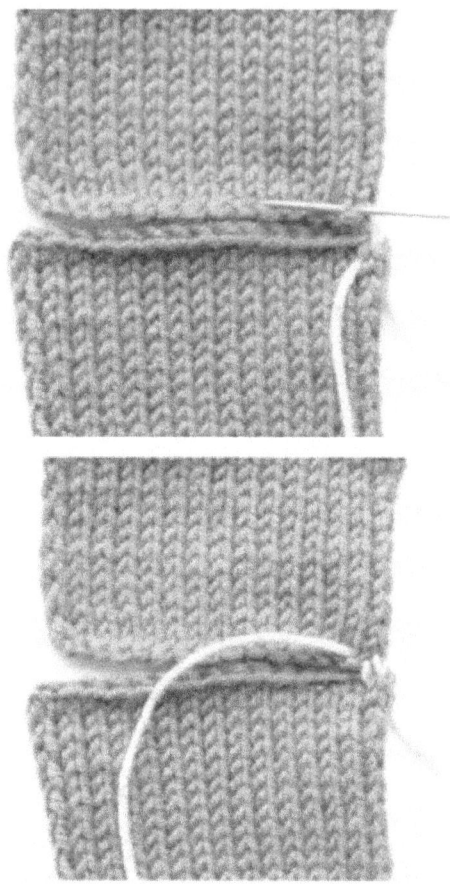

6. Proceed in this manner, working into the middle of the lower piece's stitch and beneath the top piece's stitch. A row of knit stitches will begin to appear.

While working, do not overtighten the seam; the seam's height should match the height of your usual knit stitch.

A Short message from the Author:

Hey, I hope you are enjoying the book? I would love to hear your thoughts!

Many readers do not know how hard reviews are to come by and how much they help an author.

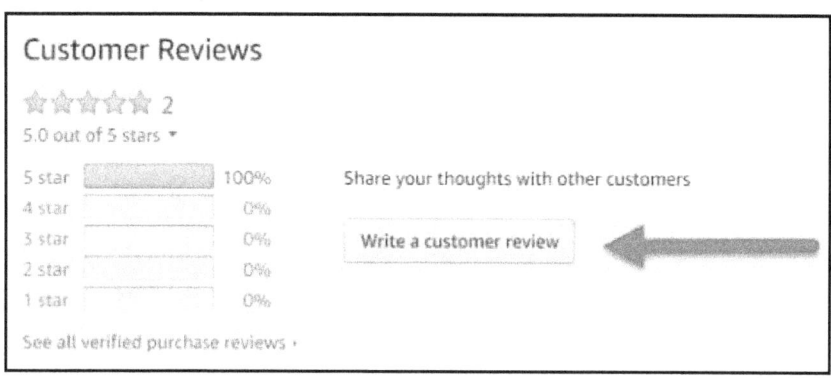

I would be incredibly grateful if you could take just 60 seconds to write a short review on Amazon, even if it is a few sentences!

>> Click here to leave a quick review

Thanks for the time taken to share your thoughts!

Chapter 4

Circular Knitting Tips and Troubleshooting

Use Different Colors of Stitch Markers

When you knit in the round, using stitch markers to mark the first stitch is essential since this indicates when a round ends and another starts. Stitch markers can also be used to highlight other aspects of your pattern, such as decreases or cables. Choose distinct colors (or objects) if you intend using more than one to not get confused while knitting.

Caste Onto a Needle

Cast your stitches on a needle, dividing them across several needles if you are knitting with double-pointed needles in the round. It's difficult to juggle all the needles on the first row, but having to simplify the cast-on could save you some stress.

A Better Join

The traditional method some knitters knit the round's first stitch can be loose and sloppy. This can be firmed up with the tail when the end is weaved in afterward.

Casting on an additional stitch may be a better technique to join it in the round. This slip should be slipped to the left, which is the first needle if using a double point needle to cast on; this is the round's starting point, and it is close to the first stitch already cast on. The two stitches should be knit altogether.

Even better, the first stitch you cast on should be slipped to the right, close to the final cast-on stitch. Slide the final cast-on stitch (presently the second stitch on the right) over the slipped stitch, tug on the yarn, and start your round.

Switching from Circular Needle to Double Point Needle

When decreasing in some cases, such as a hat's crown, you may need to switch from circular needle to double points since the number of stitches on the circular needle may no longer fit without it being stretched. Although the whole hat can be knit on a double-point needle, many people prefer circulars because they eliminate the need to juggle numerous needles.

To switch needles, simply work the subsequent round using your double point needle. The number of stitches worked by 3 or 4 needles can be divided to establish in advance the number of stitches each needle should have or simply knit and amend later by sliding stitches onto multiple needles.

Avoiding Ladders

Knitting and ladders do not complement. Ladders here refer to the annoying pesky ladders that appear when you knit circularly. Ladders are elastic stitches that are created when your stitches split very often between needles. Ladders may appear to be a dropped stitch at times, but do not be misled.

In the picture above, notice the horizontal bars that appear between the stitches. That is a ladder. Ladders are a constant issue for those practicing the magic loop, but they also appear when knitting with double-pointed needles, where they are at an increased risk of happening due to the changes in needle that occur quite too often.

Fortunately, avoiding these ladders requires only a few minor modifications. Let us examine some of the alternatives to avoiding ladders.

1. Pull the Second Stitch Firmly

Several knitters fix the problem of ladders by pulling tightly on the first stitch on the fresh needle. However, tightening the second stitch could help balance out the tension and prevent laddering.

Ladders can be formed by loose and tight tension, which is what several knitters are unaware of. In certain cases, pulling tightly on the first stitch before you move on can cause the join between the needles to become a bit too tight. The join's tension, as a result, is thrown off by the firmness of the first stitch, creating a ladder.

If you are pulling firmly on the working yarn but still have a ladder, work on leveling out the tension.

2. Don't Tug Too Tightly Before You Switch To a Fresh Needle

This issue is particular to the magic loop method. The cables on circular needles are substantially thinner compared to the needle tip. Now, if the working yarn is tightened before beginning to work on the needle nearest to you, you will be tightening the stitch to fit around the cable instead of the needle tip.

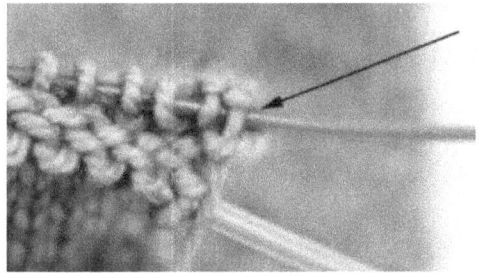

Pulling very tightly, as with the first option above, may knock off the tension of the whole round, causing ladders. Rather than tugging tightly, ensure the stitches are similar in size and tension.

3. Ensure the Stitches are Close to One Another

The space between the rear and front needle where the knitting of the next stitch occurs is seen in the above below. Once you begin to knit on a fresh needle, pinch the rear cable to meet the fresh needle, which will bridge the gap, helping you to prevent ladders.

This technique can also be used with double-pointed needles. Ensure the old, and new needles are near to each other before switching to a new double-pointed needle. This typically involves ensuring your needles are at an angle for double-pointed needles.

4. Use Another Fiber

Cotton, for example, does not have lots of elasticity. In such a case, it's uncertain that the ladder will bounce back into place after it has formed. On the other hand, wool is known for being bouncy, meaning it's more forgiving. (Read the next option if you used a bouncy yarn such as wool and still have ladders)

5. Block It

If your ladder only appears on a few occasions during the project and is not too big, blocking could help sort out this issue. As you may know, blocking forms and enables the stitches to settle. Move the stitches around when blocking your ladders to shift and conceal the ladder. Just ensure they're the same size as the rest of the stitches by adjusting them.

Be Attentive to Your Needle Length

When you knit in the round, your circular needle's length should be somewhat shorter than your piece's final circumference. For instance, if you are knitting a 40-inch waffle stitch cowl, ensure to use a 32-inch circular needle. A needle length that is longer will cause the stitches to be become too stretchy, thereby changing the gauge and altering the final piece. Conversely, using a shorter needle would not provide sufficient space to accommodate all your stitches on the cord, resulting in your piece being too small.

Have Your Tails Tightened

When your work is joined in the round, it may result in some loose stitches (or perhaps a gap) on the first row. However, this mistake can be concealed when you pull the tail tight after returning to weave the ends in; the difference will be unnoticeable.

Maintaining Straight Stitches

Ensure you maintain straight stitches when casting on. When circular and double-pointed needles are used, many knitters experience twisted stitches; so when you are done casting on, run through and straighten them out. If you have twisted cast-on stitches, it will be difficult to join your pattern, causing the remainder of your project to bend and twist in unwanted ways. Straighten your stitches upon completing every round; you will be pleased you did when you're done knitting.

Using Magic Loop for Smaller Projects

You should be familiar with the "magic loop" if you crochet, but this is a little different when you knit in the round. This " magic " will work when the cord is lengthier than the cast-on stitches number, such as for hats or sweater sleeves, this "magic" will come in handy. It essentially enables you to utilize circular needles, especially when working on smaller circumference projects. The magic loop technique is discussed extensively in chapter 5.

Keep Your Working Yarn Outside

Ensure your working yarn is on the circle's perimeter as you knit. It should run up from the last cast-on stitch rather than across the middle of the circle.

Dropped Stitches

Don't be alarmed. This occurs frequently. When your knitting is put down, a stitch could fall off, or your needle's end will come off if you don't pay close attention. Sometimes, it may work its way far down into the fabric, but the best part is that it can be fixed!

It's also simple to catch. Periodically inspect your fabric for any abnormal globules of stitches sticking out or a gaping row of ladders. Count your stitches frequently to ensure that your stitch count isn't decreasing. Always put your knitting on hold upon getting to a row's end. Cramming your knitting in your project bag in the middle of a row, for instance, is a definite way of losing stitches. Looking at your work, the dropped stitch can be seen to hang out mournfully beneath what appears to be a set of ladder rungs. These ladder rungs give rise to the working yarn from the individual row coming out of the dropped stitch. We'll reattach the lost stitch to the ladder rungs by reconstructing a stitch at every row or rung.

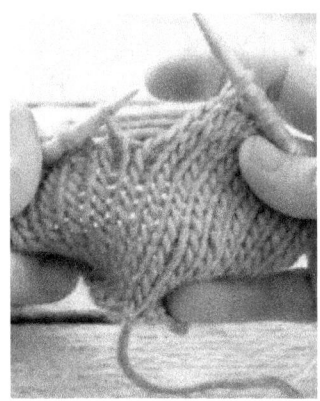

Begin by picking up the visible last stitch with your left needle. The stitch's right-hand side will be in the needle's front. The working yarn ladder rungs from the rows where the stitch dropped will dangle above it.

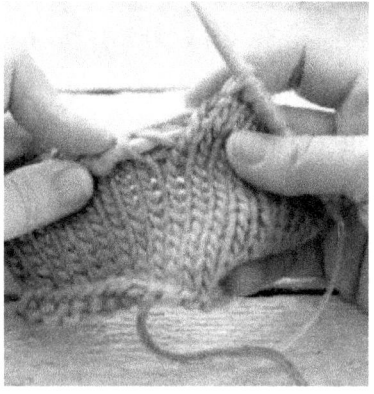

Now, run your left needle beneath the lowest rung of the ladder.

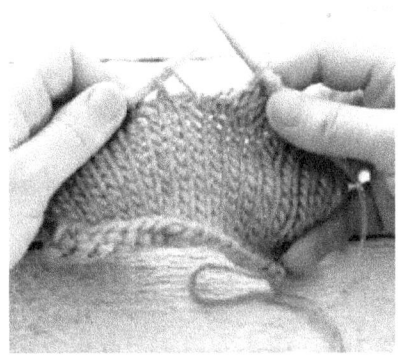

You will have the former stitch as well as the ladder rung (working yarn) from the row that is atop your needle's dropped stitch.

Slip your right needle into the dropped stitch, pulling it across the first rung of ladder that's on your needle. You've successfully picked up a stitch for a row. Insert your left needle beneath the next accessible rung of ladder and repeat the above procedures to reconstruct the stitch for that row.

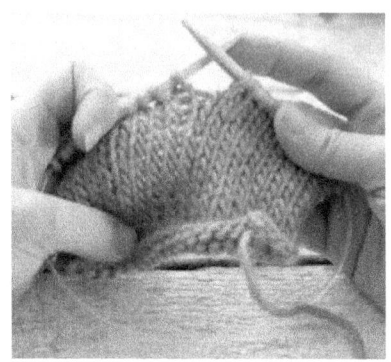

Continue pulling the stitch up at every row, reconstructing the stitch as demonstrated above till you get to the top. That row of stitches may appear a bit loose at first; however, it will become less visible as you continue working and blocking your work.

Extra Stitches

Accidental yarnovers and knitting into the gaps among stitches are the two most prevalent causes of extra stitches. When your yarn is brought to your work's front (in contrast to leaving it at the back), you get an accidental yarn over. As you proceed to knit the subsequent stitch, the working yarn then shoots up and over your needle, forming an additional loop on your needle.

Sometimes, you unknowingly find yourself knitting in the gap between two stitches. The image below shows that the needle doesn't go across an old stitch; instead, it goes below the previous row's working yarn, resulting in an extra stitch.

Looking at your fabric often for any bizarre-shaped holes or spots in which the stitch does not feel right is the simplest way to detect extra stitches. An accidental yarn over can be seen from the purl side in the picture below. Also, keep track of your stitches constantly; your stitch count will increase if extra stitches are added.

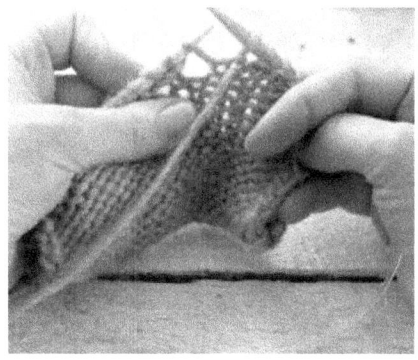

The best approach to fixing an extra stitch problem is determined by its location. If the extra stitch was introduced inside the past 1-2 rows, the simplest solution is to pluck the extra stitches from your needle. The working yarn in the 1-2 rows would be a bit loose, and you may end up with a larger-looking stitch, but it would still be manageable compared to a big hole.

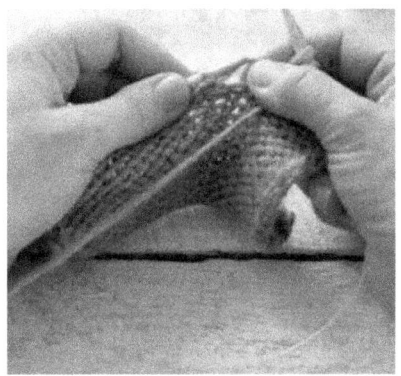

If the problematic extra stitch was recently added, knit backward stitch after stitch to get to the problematic stitch. Insert your left needle beneath the last finished stitch (as shown below) and bring out the working yarn while transferring the stitch from the right to the left needle.

If the problematic extra stitch occurred a while ago, you could choose to tear out your knitting until the problematic stitch is removed. Remove your work from the needles and place it on a flat surface. The working yarn should gradually be taken off the stitches till the extra stitch is undone.

Pick up the stitches after you've torn your knitting; the stitch's right half should be in the needle's front. Do not stress if one of the stitches is pulled down another row; simply place the last noticeable stitch on the needle, mark its position, and continue. Return to where the dropped stitch is upon picking up the entire row of stitches. Just adopt your new method of picking up dropped stitches from the picture below.

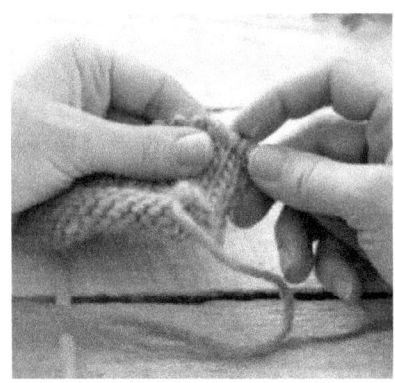

My Cast-On Round Has a Gap

There's a range of methods you can cast on to avoid the gap. One way to do this after you bind off is to grab either a tapestry needle or crochet hook and then pull your yarn's tail through the round's first stitch. If you pull it a little tighter and weave in that end, no one will know a gap ever existed there.

For future purposes, you can easily adopt several ways to begin knitting on circular needles to prevent the gap, like casting on with an invisible join or starting your round when you knit some stitches with your working yarn and tail. The latter has the advantage of weaving your tail in for you, but the disadvantage is that it makes it more difficult to spot the start of your round if your stitch marker is ever lost.

Chapter 5

Circular Knitting Techniques

Long Tail Cast On

Cast-on stitches in the round is similar to that of flat knitting. Learning how to knit with a long tail cast on is a crucial skill to master. You will be relieved to learn that casting on for circular knitting is simple to do.

A circular cast-on is quite essential in starting a top-down hat, center-out shawl, or toe-up sock. A circular needle or DPNs can be used to cast on; nevertheless, the cast-on in the instructions below was made with a circular needle.

Procedure

1. To get started, tie a slip knot and slip it into one needle, holding it in your right hand

2. With the two yarns placed on your left hand, wrap the yarn tail across your left thumb plus the working yarn across your left index finger. This should give rise to the shape "V," with the left of your palm facing you.

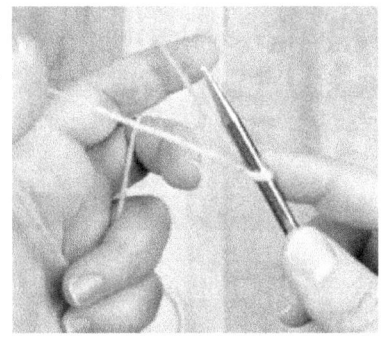

3. As illustrated below, the yarn should be pulled from beneath your thumb with your right needle's tip.

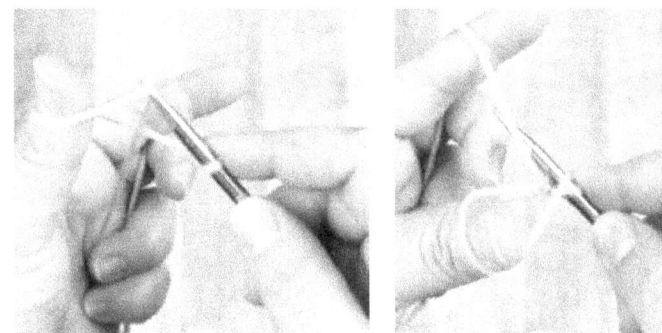

4. Then, move right, beneath your index finger's yarn and go back via your thumb's loop as given below.

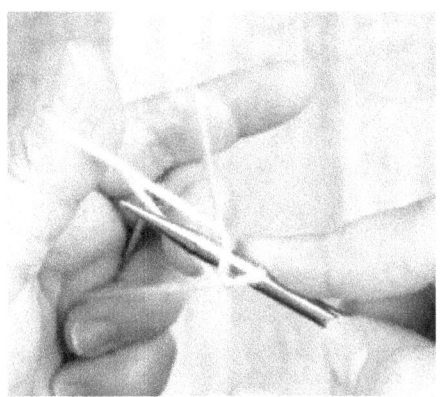

5. The image below depicts the yarn being released from the thumb. The new stitch will be on the right needle, and now, you can have it tightened on the needle.

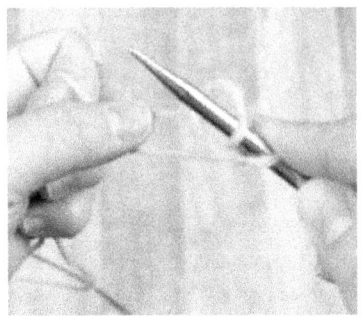

6. Repeat steps 3-5 until you've cast on the required number of stitches.

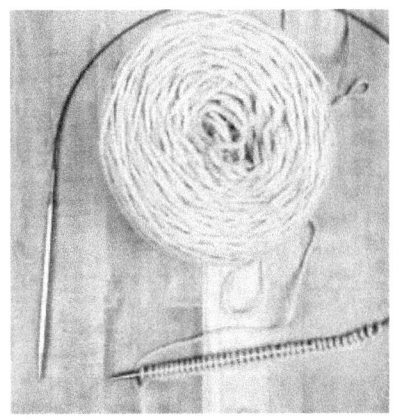

Joining In The Round

Connecting the first and last cast-on stitches altogether is how to join when knitting in the round. Circular knitting is made feasible when stitches are joined. But first, you would cast on stitches before joining your knitting in the round. In this case, you will cast on as usual (we just covered the long tail cast on), but if you are following a particular knitting pattern outside this book, ensure to double-check the cast-on method and stitch count.

Before you join the round, ensure you don't have twisted stitches (earlier, we discussed some tips around keeping your stitches straight before joining in the round). Before starting the joining process, double-check that your cast-on row is straight. If your stitches are twisted and you want to knit a hat, you will need to start anew. Nobody enjoys doing that. Although a few patterns, such as the Mobius Cowl, benefit from a twisted cast-on, most patterns require that your cast-on be straightened out before you join.

Procedure

- Examine your stitches to ensure that your cast-on row is straight. You don't want to knit with twisted stitches (we have overemphasized this enough).
- Arrange your needles, as shown in the image below. The last cast-on stitch would be on the right needle, whereas the first cast-on stitch would be on the left needle.

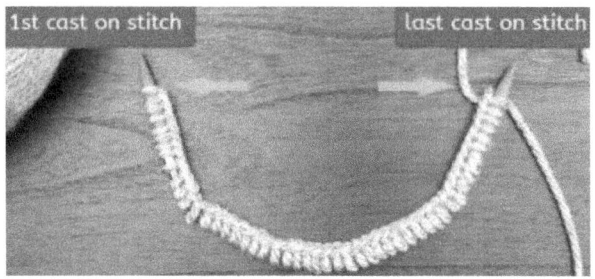

This is the arrangement you'll always adopt for your knitting needles for a round join

Now, below are the different techniques for joining your knitting in the round.

Technique 1: Stitch Swap Join

1. To begin, make a long tail stitch cast on (per the number of stitches your project needs).
2. Then, slip your right needle in the first stitch to your left side. The stitch should be slipped as though you're purling.

3. Then, slide your left needle in your right needle's last cast-on stitch. This stitch should be passed across to the other.

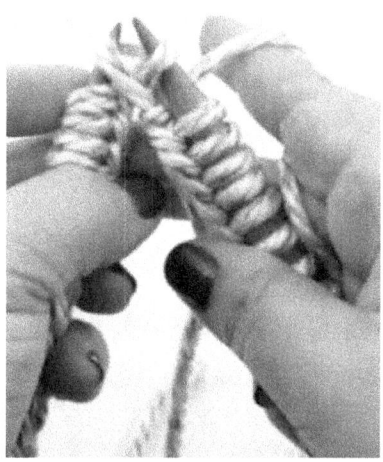

Tip: Ensure your yarn is at the front and (or rear) of your needles and prepared to begin knitting (or purling) your first stitch.

4. Start knitting in the round by inserting your right needle into your left needle's first stitch.

Technique 2: Add 1, Decrease 1 Join

1. An extra stitch should be added to your cast-on row when casting on, then purlwise transfer the extra stitch to the needle on the left.

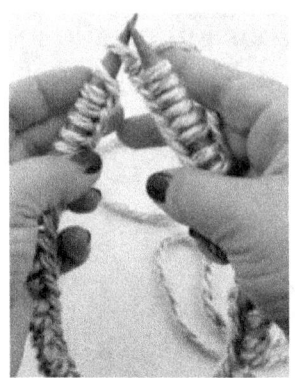

2. Knit two together (k2tog) using the needle on the right. Keep knitting after that.

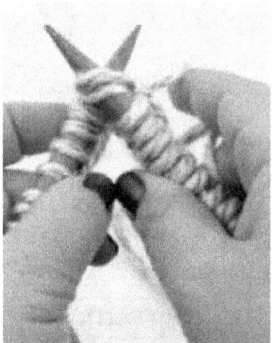

Tip: Use a stitch marker to indicate the start of your round.

Technique 3: Invisible Join

Using this technique, you'd have to cast on one more stitch than your pattern demands.

1. To start, purlwise transfer the first stitch from the needle on your left to the needle on your right.

2. Now, drop the extra stitch from the needle by passing it across the slipped stitch. An increased stitch is visible in the picture below; however, this will subsequently be fixed in another step.

3. Then, slip your right needle's first stitch back to your left needle.

4. Tighten the extra yarn with the working yarn and yarn tail, making the join invisible.
5. Finally, go ahead to knit in the round.

Tip: Tighten the join well enough upon returning to the start of the round. This will help you prevent a gap in your knitting to make a smooth, seamless join.

Binding Off

You must bind off (cast off) your piece once you have finished knitting in the round; this ensures your knitting does not unravel. The basic bind-off is among the easiest and most popular bind-offs, which is what is covered below. One circular needle is used in the traditional way to bind off, as shown below.

1. A stitch marker should be placed on the needle to your right to mark a round's end. Then, as is customary, the round's first two stitches should be knitted.

You currently have two stitches on your right needle to the end-of-the-round marker's left. Note that I used a different yarn color to indicate which stitches I'm working but ensure you use your project's yarn color when binding off

2. Use your left needle's tip to push the right needle's first stitch of the round up and across the second stitch and away from the right needle.

With this, one stitch is now bound off with one stitch remaining on the right needle to the end-of-round marker's left.

3. One extra stitch should be knitted, giving rise to two stitches on the needle to the right hand and to the end-of-the-round marker's left. The first stitch should now be pulled across the second stitch and away from the right needle. Repeat until you've completed the round with only one stitch left on your right needle.

If the pattern says "bind off in pattern," rather than having to knit every stitch before you bind off, simply knit or purl as needed to keep the stitch pattern going.

4. Leave an 8" tail when cutting the yarn. Remove the last loop from the needle and push it up until the yarn's tail is free and the loop is not present anymore.

The stitches that are bound off will look like a sequence of overlaying Vs running horizontally along your work's edge.

5. Now, the tail of the yarn should be threaded onto a seaming needle. Slip the seaming needle from the front to the back beneath the two legs of the V that produces the first round's bound-off stitch. The needle should be pulled through the stitch and tightened.

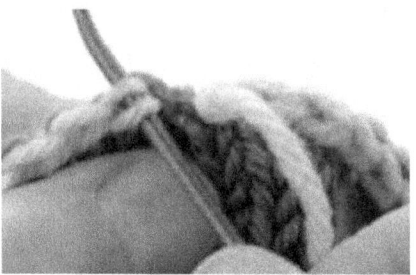

Be careful not to stretch the fabric by pulling it too tight.

6. The seaming needle should be inserted down into the last bound-off stitch's center (i.e., into the "V's" center) and then back into the project's center.

   The needle should now be pulled across and snugged up the yarn such that the connecting stitch is similar in size to the bound-off stitches around it

7. As usual, weave the yarn tail in on the fabric's wrong side.

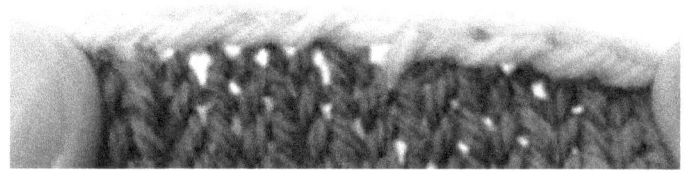

To get a bound-off edge that is loose, the bind-off should be worked with a needle bigger in size (either one or two inches bigger) than the needle utilized in making your project.

Working With Double Pointed Needles

Double pointed needles (DPNs) are ideal for making several projects like hats and socks. Although they may appear overwhelming at first, they're actually fairly easy to use. Knitting with DPNs is the same as knitting with two needles after joining in the round.

Steps

Casting On

1. When working with any particular pattern outside this book, ensure to read the pattern's requirements for the number of DPNs you'll need. Many patterns call for knitting on four needles, while the fifth needle will be used in performing the actual knitting. Nevertheless,

certain patterns only call for three needles, while the fourth needle will be used in performing the actual knitting.

Packs of five DPNs are commonly sold. As with normal needles, they come with numbers, so ensure you pick the correct size.

2. On one needle, use the long-tail cast-on method to cast on the desired stitch count. After that, take one of your DPNs, and cast all the stitches on it.

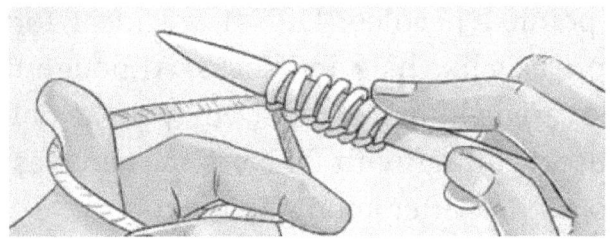

You'd need to be able to shift the stitches around, so do not cast on too tightly.

3. If you are making use of four needles, half of the stitches should be slipped onto a second needle. The needle that has all the stitches should be held in your left hand. In your right hand, a second needle should be held. Now, half of the stitches should be pulled off the first needle using the second needle.

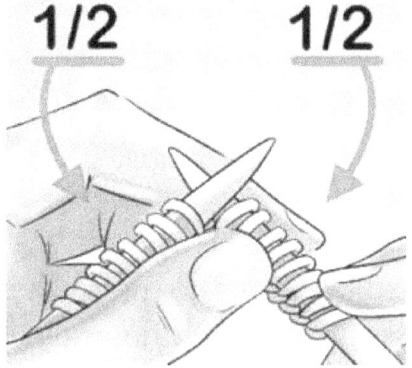

Continue in this manner until the stitches on each needle are even in number. For instance, if 32 stitches were cast on, each needle would have 16 stitches.

4. If three needles are being used, 1/3 of the stitches should be slipped onto a second needle. Now, use your left hand to hold the needle with the stitches and your right hand to hold the second needle. 1/3 of the stitches from the first needle should be picked up with the second needle.

   For instance, if 18 stitches were cast on, then only 6 will be slipped off. On one needle, 12 stitches will be present, and on the other, 6 stitches.

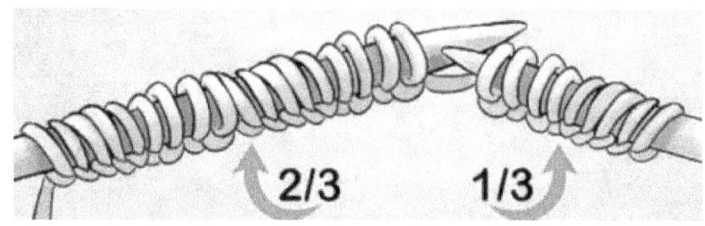

5. Keep distributing the stitches evenly across the other needles. Move to the second needle's right side and take half of the stitches with a third needle. Proceed to the left of your first needle and take half of the stitches with a fourth needle. For instance, if 32 stitches were cast on, then you will have 8 stitches on each needle.

If you are using three needles to knit, simply return to the first needle's left side and take 1/3 of the stitches. For instance, if 18 stitches were cast on, your needle will contain 6 stitches.

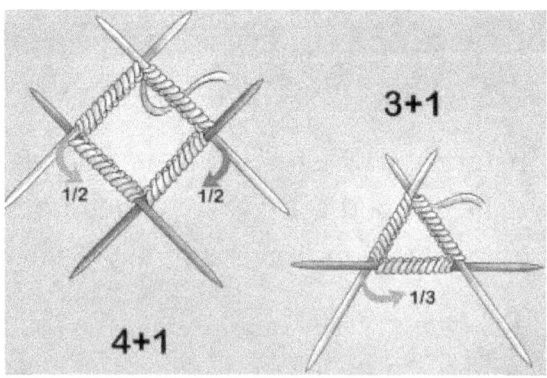

6. A stitch marker should be placed among your needle's last two stitches. Doing this will help you to identify the row's end. Although this isn't strictly necessary, it will make it much easier to know when a row ends and another begins.

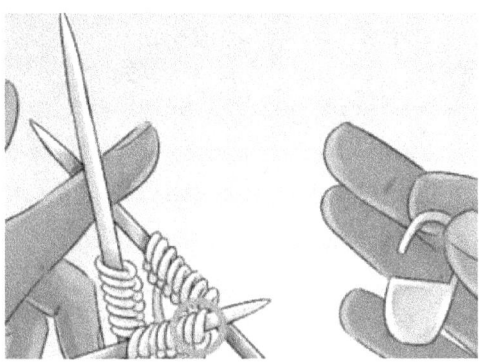

If stitch markers aren't available, a loosely different yarn color should be tied around the needle among the last two stitches.

Joining in the Round

Steps

1. The needle with the working yarn should be held in your right hand. Usually, you would knit using the working yarn in your left hand; however, for this, you should use your right. Ensure the stitches are near to the needle's tip.

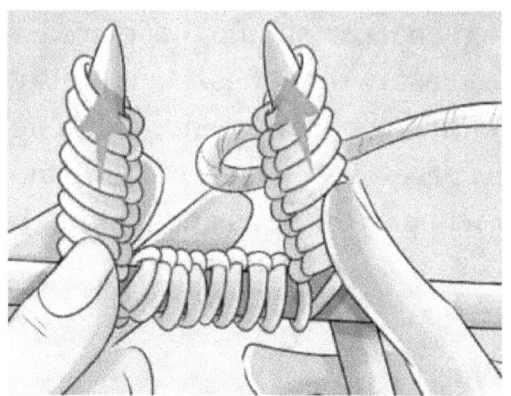

To knit using your left hand, that needle should be switched to your right

2. The last needle should be inserted into the first stitch. Hold your fourth (if you are using three needles) or fifth (if you are using four needles) needle with your right hand and have its tip inserted into your left needle's first stitch.

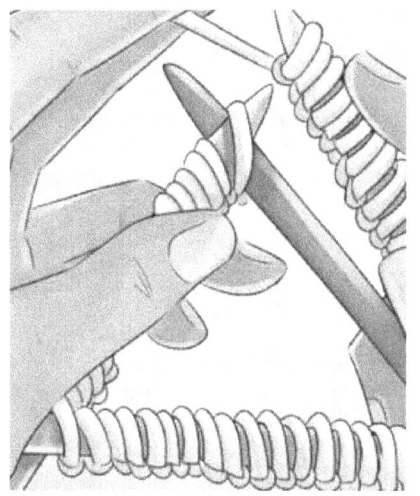

Ensure the needle goes across your work's front and exits at the back Just as you knit (not purl).

The needle needs to be held in your ring and pinky fingers with the working yarn loosely tied to it.

3. The working yarn should be wrapped around the right needle's tip. The needle with the working yarn should now be turned towards the left needle to create a square (if using four needles) or a triangle (if using three needles). Now, the working yarn should be wrapped around the right needle's tip.

Do not simply lay the yarn over the needle's tip. The yarn should be wrapped around the tip of the right needle and draped over the top and side.

4. The yarn should be pulled across the stitch and then slipped off the stitch. Pull the looped yarn across the first stitch with the right needle's tip. Slip the first stitch away from the left needle after ensuring the looped yarn is on the right needle.

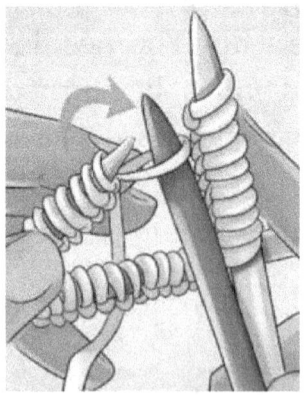

Nothing is to be added to the needle with your working yarn. To retain your appearance, ensure the needle is kept near to the left needle.

5. Keep a tight square or triangular structure by tugging on the yarn. When working with DPNs, it's crucial to knitting securely in the corners. The original needles should be moved around until your square or triangle has a tight corner, then tug on the yarn for necessary adjustment.

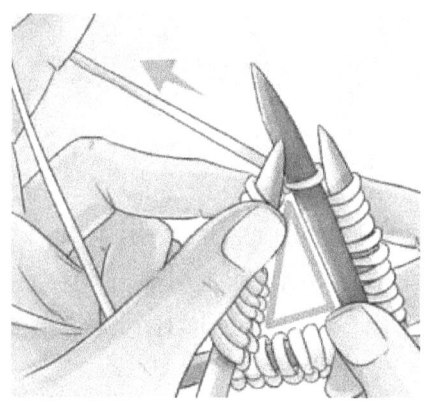

You would have five needles in the form of a hexagon if you began with four.

You would have four needles in the form of a square if you began with three.

Knitting and Completing Your Project

1. Knit across the first needle as normal. After joining in the round, the first needle can be knitted across as you would on a pair of standard needles. Stop after you've gotten to the first needle's end.

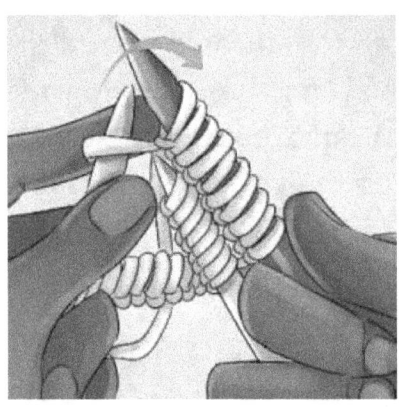

   This tutorial centers on a simple knitting pattern. If you have any pattern that demands for a combination of several stitches, then go with your pattern.

2. The subsequent set of stitches should be knitted with a fresh empty needle. Upon knitting all the stitches off the first needle, the second needle will now be full and with an empty first needle. This fresh empty needle should now be knitted over the second needle's stitches. Ensure the new

needle's fresh stitch is tight to avoid gaps or laddering.

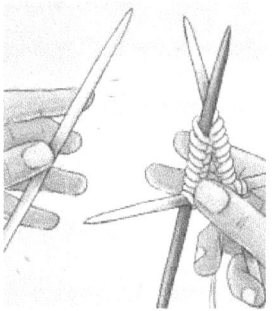

3. Proceed in this way until you return to your starting point. You'll have an empty needle once you've finished knitting every side of your triangle or square. With this needle, go ahead to knit the stitches off the subsequent needle.

Ensure every corner is tightly knitted.

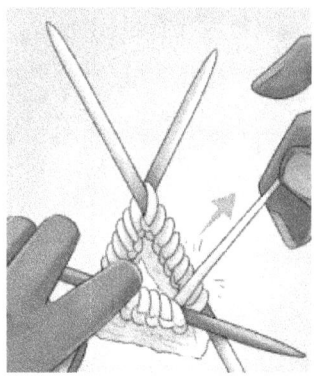

4. Complete the last stitch by sliding the stitch marker onto your needle. Knitting on DPNs is comparable to when you knit in the round, i.e., your project does not need to be turned. The stitch marker should be slipped onto your right needle after finishing the second-to-last stitch, then finish the last stitch.

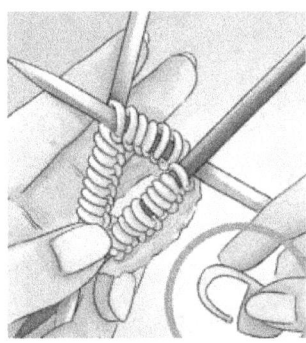

Your first row is now complete.

5. Begin a second row without turning, then continue to knit. Your stitches do not need to be turned or reversed. Simply do as the pattern directs, remembering to count a fresh row after repositioning your stitch marker and completing the last stitch.

147

The piece you are knitting might not appear as you desire at first, but it will begin to take shape after a few rows.

Working With One Circular Needle: Traditional Way

When you adopt the traditional way of knitting circularly using just one circular knitting needle, you will cast your stitches on the circular needle and have them distributed equally onto the whole needle, sliding them along the cord or cable while working in a continual loop around the surrounding of your piece.

Steps

1. With your desired method for casting on (long tail for simplicity), cast your stitches onto the circular needle.

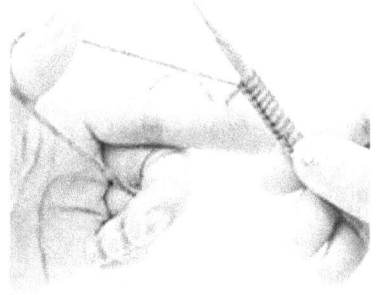

2. Take note of the braided edging that runs all the way of the cast on.

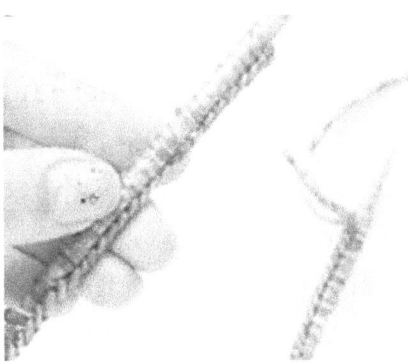

3. The braided edge should be turned such that it faces the same direction. The stitches will not twist as a result of this.

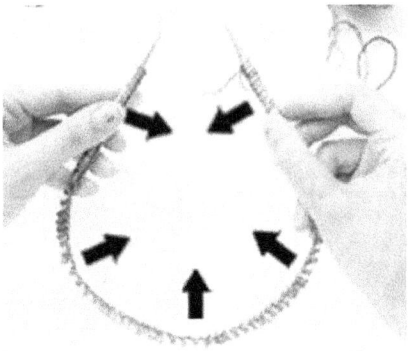

4. Ensure that the working yarn is on the appropriate needle. A stitch marker should be placed on the right-hand needle

5. Prepare to knit by bringing the stitches nearer to the needle's tip.

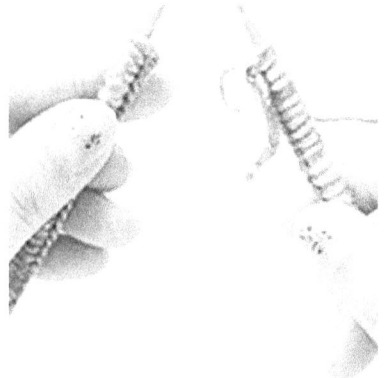

6. The right needle should be used to knit into the left needle's first stitch

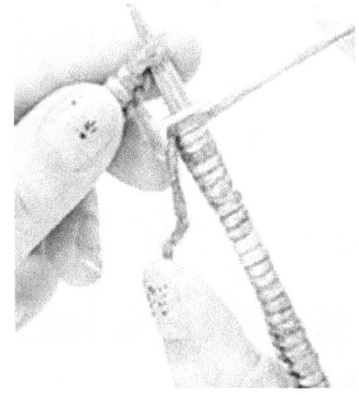

7. From the left needle, the first stitch should be knitted and tightened. With this, you have succeeded in joining your stitches in the round. We discussed techniques of joining in the round earlier; ensure you revisit that section.

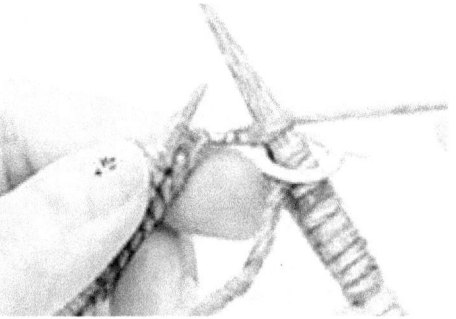

8. From the left needle, the second stitch should be knitted. Keep knitting all the way of the entire round.

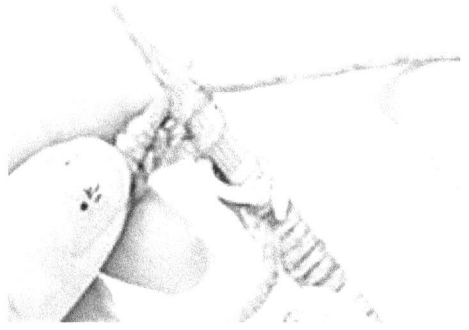

9. Keep knitting after slipping the marker to the right-hand needle at the round's end.

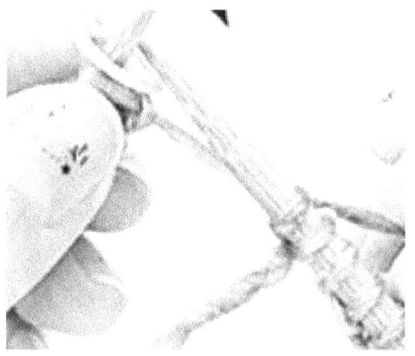

10. Your piece will resemble the image below after many rounds of knitting.

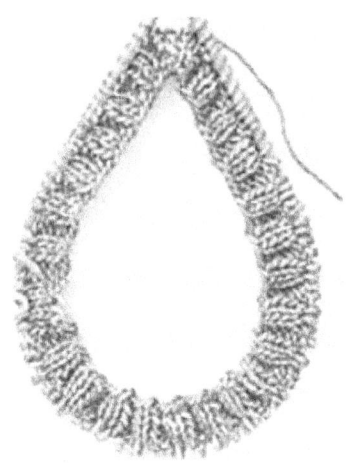

11. When you have finished knitting, bind off and weave in the tail as earlier discussed

Working With One Long Circular Needle: Magic Loop

When it comes to knitting all those fall sweaters, you're surely aware that knitting in the round is the ultimate game-changer. However, when knitting anything that is smaller such as mittens, socks, sleeves, etc., you'll have to perform some magic. You can learn a truly magical knitting technique. The magic loop technique should be your new best pal.

How Does Magic Loop Knitting Work?

The magic loop technique involves the use of only one long, circular needle to create projects with small circumferences (such as the sleeves of sweaters or socks). The magic loop can be achieved with any size of needle but with a length of cable measuring at a minimum of 32-inches or more. So experiment with different lengths to see which one performs better for you.

Steps

1. Start by casting on the number of desired stitches.

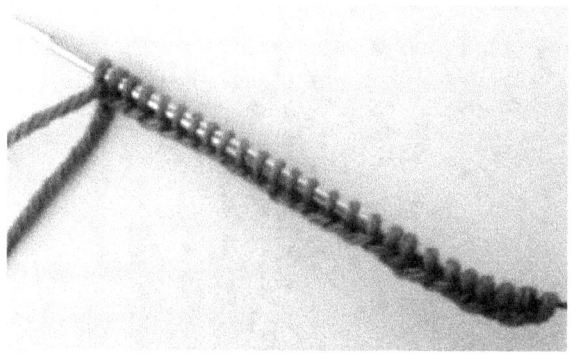

2. Locate the center point of the cable by moving the stitches to the middle of the cable (simply count to locate the center of the cable). Bring your cable up between the two middle stitches by gently bending it.

3. Gently pull the cable until the cast-on stitches are lying on the needles (not the cable).

4. Ensure the needles are parallel to the ground after turning them. The nearest needle closer to you should accommodate the first cast-on stitch. The yarn's tail should be hung down, and then the working yarn should be laid across the back needle.

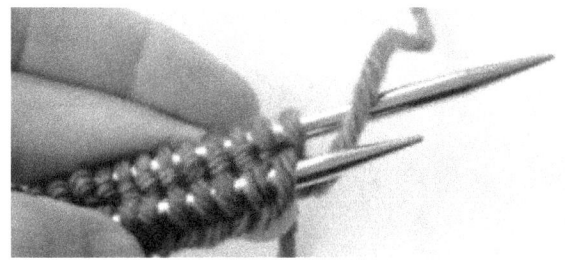

Tip: This will prepare you to knit your first stitch. If your first stitch is being purled, your working yarn should be allowed to dangle downward among the needles.

5. Pull out the back needle such that the cable accommodates the back stitches. Ensure the working yarn is kept behind the work. To knit, the needle should be inserted into the first stitch.

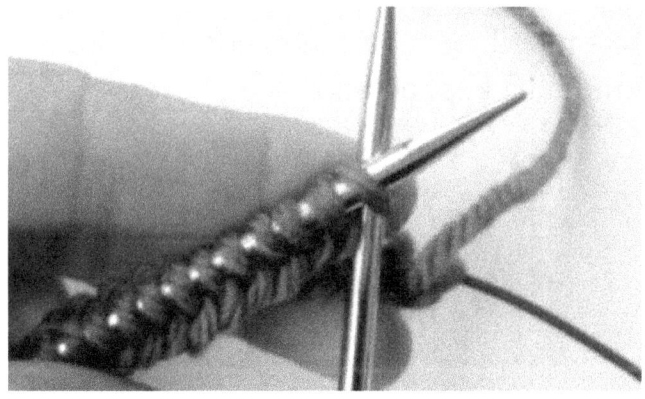

6. All stitches should be knitted on the front needle

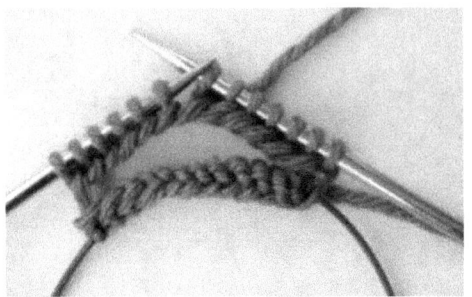

7. After you've finished the first pair, your needles should be turned such that the stitches yet to be worked are nearest to you.

The back needle should be pulled (which you recently worked on) so that the stitches you just worked on are resting on the cable. Then, the unworked stitches should be slipped on the front needle. Then, the unworked stitches should ` be slipped on the front needle. The working yarn should be kept behind.

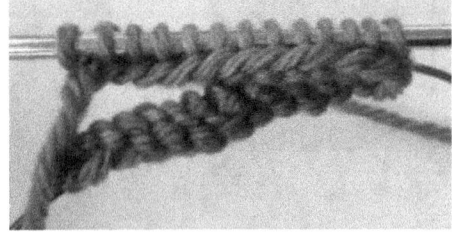

8. Move the back needle over and begin knitting the first stitch on the front needle.

Ensure to knit in the pattern all through to the front needle. Knit in the pattern on the front needle all the way down. You will have completed one round upon finishing this series of stitches.

9. Carry on in this manner for as many rounds as required by the pattern you are working with. There you have it; your magic loop!

The end... almost!

Hey! We've made it to the final chapter of this book, and I hope you've enjoyed it so far.

If you have not done so yet, I would be incredibly thankful if you could take just a minute to leave a quick review on Amazon

Reviews are not easy to come by, and as an independent author with a little marketing budget, I rely on you, my readers, to leave a short review on Amazon.

Even if it is just a sentence or two!

So if you really enjoyed this book, please...

>> Click here to leave a brief review on Amazon.

I truly appreciate your effort to leave your review, as it truly makes a huge difference.

Chapter 6

Circular Knitting Patterns and Projects

Congratulations on making it to this chapter. This chapter is where we will consolidate what has been previously covered into making actual modern projects; so let's get right into it. Aha! I used some abbreviations in the projects below; so ensure you refer to the list of abbreviations earlier provided if you have any challenges figuring out what each abbreviation stands for.

Hats

Tools and Materials

- A skein of super chunky or bulky yarn or a 14 ply yarn plus thick wool ease yarn of Lion brand
- A US circular needle of size 15 16" or 15 20"
- Tape measure
- Scissors
- Darning needle
- Stitch markers

Othe Tools

- Pom pom maker clover that is 2 – ½" large in size

Measurements

- Adult woman
- Length of hat laying flat without pom = 9 ½"
- Width of hat lying flat = 9 ½"
- Circumference of the head = About 22-26"

Gauge

- 10 sts and 15 rows = 4in/10cm in Stockinette stitch

Steps

Casting On

1. Use the long-tail cast-on technique discussed to cast 38 stitches onto your circulars.

After casting on 38 stitches, ensure you have the correct number of stitches.

Joining in the Round

2. Insert a place marker at the join and follow the joining-in-the-round technique earlier explained to join your stitches. Ensure the stitches are not twisted

Knitting the Rib Stitch

3. After casting on your stitches and joining in the round, knitting the ribbing is the next step. This is the hat's elastic part, making it possible to wear on and remove from your head.

The pattern below is a 1 x 1 rib stitch, where one stitch is knitted, and one stitch is purled for five rounds. Please refer to our earlier discussion in chapter 3 on knitting the rib stitch, or better still, do the following;

4. Round 1: *knit 1, purl 1; rep from * to the round's end
5. Round 2 plus every other round (6 rounds total): the knit stitches should be knitted, and the purl stitches should be purled.
6. Rep rounds 4 and 5 until you achieve your desired length

Knitting the Hat's Body

The remainder of the design is rather simple once you've finished the ribbing. You'd use the knit stitch in knitting all subsequent rounds. This is the easiest section of the hat to make - see the pattern as follows;

7. Round 7: Knit
8. Round 7 should be repeated (knit each round) until the piece has a measurement of 8-inches from the cast-on edge.

   There will be more droop on the hat the lengthier it is made.

   The hat's size is 8 inches long; however, it can be made longer or shorter based on how fitting or droopy you want it.

Completing the Hat

To finish the hat, decrease it using K2tog, which is a very simple reduction method.

Knitting two stitches together, or K2tog, is a typical method of decreasing stitches.

Casting off is not required in this case; just thread a long yarn tail via the extra stitches, pull them together, and secure them.

We discussed how to decrease stitches earlier. But for this project, follow the pattern's decreasing instructions below;

9. K1, K2tog – repeat to the round's end – to the last two stitches, K2
10. Knit to the round's end
11. K2tog, K1 – repeat to the round's end
12. Cut the yarn
13. Pull the end via the remaining stitches and fasten off
14. Loose ends should be sewn in

Stitching the Pom Pom

Pull the long yarn tail via the hat's top after you've closed and fastened the top.

Make a pom-pom using a pom pom maker or from cardboard. Here, a clover of 2 – ½" large was utilized.

Follow the instructions below to attach the pom-pom to the hat's top:

15. The needle should be pushed via the pom-poms' center with the yarn sticking out of the hat's top.
16. It should be pushed back via the pom-pom and into the top of the hat's center.

17. Repeat step 16 twice or more, then hide the stitches that go through the pom-pom.
18. After it seems secure, the inside of the hat's top should be fastened with a knot
19. Any loose ends should be weaved in; snip the yarn

Weaving the Ends In

20. Some loose ends will need some weaving in. i.e., from the hat's cast-on and the sewing of the pom-pom into position. To accomplish this, have them weaved along the stitch's edge, where they will be concealed and unable to come off. Take out the stitch marker and test your hat

That's about it!

Headband

Tools and Materials

- 60g DK or light worsted yarn (cat no. 3) in a lighter hue was used for the band. A 10g DK or light worsted yarn (cat no. 3) in a darker hue was used for the knot.
- US circular knitting needle of size 80cm/32 inches or longer was used. DPNs can be used instead.
- Tapestry needle

Measurements

- This headband is designed to fit a woman's medium head circumference (about 54-56cm/21-22 inches), although it can be adjusted easily
- More or lesser stitches should be cast on if you desire to adjust the headband's width.
- Knit lesser or more rows if you want the circumference to be lesser or larger.
- 10cm (4 inches) wide by 24.5cm (9.6 inches) long is the finished size.

Gauge

- 26 sts and 32 rows = 10x10cm (4x4 inches) in Stockinette stitch upon blocking

Steps

Casting On

1. Use a light yarn color to cast on 50 stitches using the long-tail technique.

Joining in the Round

Use the magic loop technique to join in the round:

2. Bring the stitches to the cable's center, and fold the cable halfway, pulling it across the middle of the stitches. Half of the stitches should be placed on the front needle and the other half on the back needle.

3. Remove the needle holding the yarn tail such that the stitches are resting on the cable.

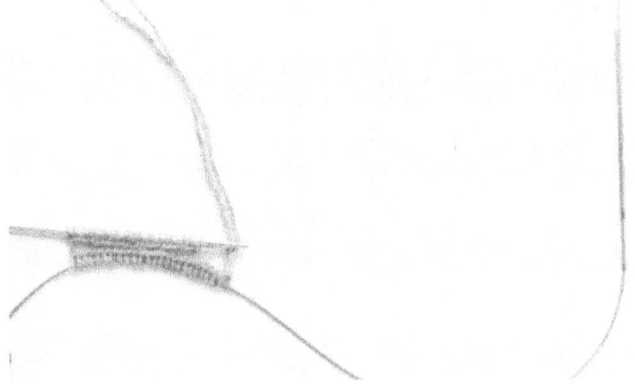

4. Ensure the stitches are not twisted, indicate the start of a new round with a stitch marker, and begin knitting.

Making the Band

5. Knit in stockinette stitch until the headband has a measurement of around 50 cm (19.7 inches) long or until the target length is reached.

Binding off

6. Knit two stitches - with two stitches on your right needle, slip the left needle into the right needle's first stitch, bringing it over the second stitch. Your right needle has one stitch left.

7. Knit one stitch – with two stitches on your right needle again, slip the left needle into the right needle's first stitch, bringing it over the first stitch. Your right needle has one stitch left.

8. Step 7 should be repeated until you get to the round's end.

9. Snip the yarn once there is just one stitch left, and leave a of about 80cm (32 inches) for the edges to be seamed together. The yarn should be pulled via the last stitch.

Seaming

10. Use the horizontal mattress stitch earlier discussed in chapter 3 to have both the cast-on and bind-off edges seamed. Do not be worried if the seam is imperfect, because the knot or middle part will conceal it.

    The edges of the headband should folded. The cast-on edge should be above the bind-off (i.e., the section that has the tails of the yarn)

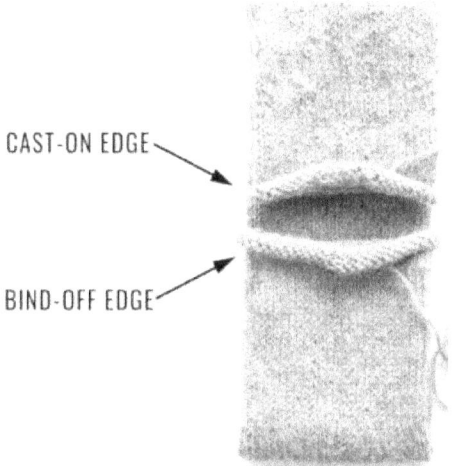

CAST-ON EDGE

BIND-OFF EDGE

11. Find the first stitch, which should be right above the cast-on edge. The yarn should be pulled through by inserting the needle beneath that stitch (below the two legs of the "V").

12. Now find the first stitch, which should be directly beneath the bind-off edge. Your needle should be inserted via that first stitch's middle (i.e., front to back, into the "Vs" middle), bringing it up via the next stitch's middle (i.e., front to back)

13. Steps 11 and 12 should be repeated all-around - work beneath the top piece stitch and into the middle of the lower piece stitches. Upon completion, you'd have something like the one shown below

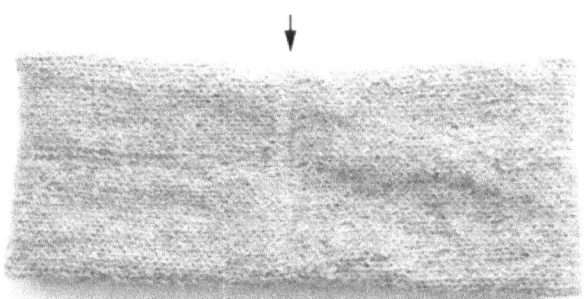

Middle Section

The middle section is worked like that of the headband, only smaller.

14. Cast on 24 stitches using a darker yarn, and use the magic loop technique to join in the round. Afterward, knit using the stockinette stitch for 10cm (4 inches), then bind off.

Assembling

15. The headband should be placed alongside the seam right in the center and pressed a bit. Afterward, the middle section should be placed between the layers, casting on edge right above the edge of the bind-off.

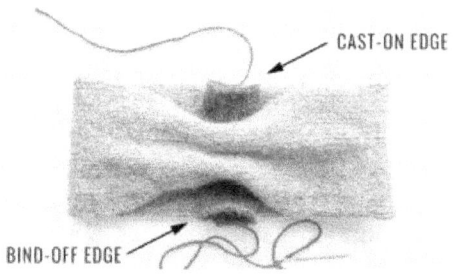

CAST-ON EDGE

BIND-OFF EDGE

16. The middle section of the tube should be wrapped around the headband and use the horizontal mattress stitch in seaming the edges of the tube's cast-on and bind-off, just as you did with the headband.

17. As you seam, the edges of the middle section should be moved to the right.

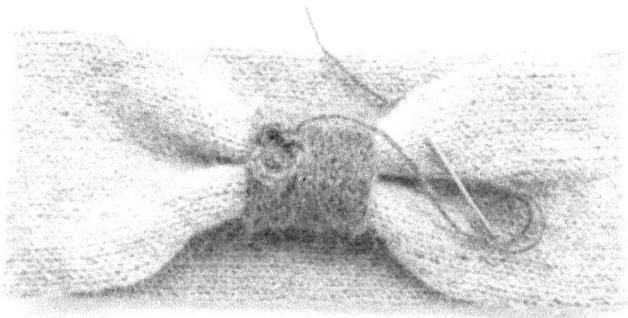

Once you've completed weaving the loose ends in, the knot should be turned such that the seam is concealed in the back.

And you're done!

Cable Cowl

Tools and Materials

- A worsted weight yarn of 85g (3 oz) / medium (cat no. 4) merino wool
- Circular knitting needles of sizes 4.5mm (US7) and 5mm (US8) 40cm (16 inches).
- Cable needle or substituted with a double-pointed needle or a large safety pin.
- Tapestry needle
- Stitch marker
- Scissors

Measurements

Completed upon blocking:

- Circumference: 48cm (18.9 inches)
- Height: 30cm (11 inches)

If you prefer changing the cowl's circumference, fewer or more stitches should be cast on. A repeat of one pattern is approximately 9cm (3.5 inches).

Gauge

- 24 sts x 26 rows = 10 x 10cm (4 x 4 inches) in pattern upon blocking

Note This

- Cable 2 Back (C2B) – Slip one stitch onto the cable needle and place it at the rear of the work. The subsequent stitch should be knitted, and after that, the stitch should be knitted from the cable needle.
- Cable 2 Front (C2F) – Slip one stitch onto the cable needle and place it in front of the work. The subsequent stitch should be knitted, and after that, the stitch should be knitted from the cable needle.

Steps

Casting On

1. Use the long-tail cast-on technique to cast on 120 stitches using smaller needles.

Joining in the Round

Join your stitches in the round and ensure it's not twisted; place a stitch marker therein. To join in the round, use the invisible method earlier discussed in chapter 5. But for the sake of this project, see below:

2. 120 stitches plus 1 additional stitch should be cast on (a total of 121 stitches).
3. The first stitch should be slipped purlwise from the needle on the left to that on the right.
4. The second stitch should be passed from the right needle above the first stitch (the stitch just passed from the left needle).

5. Return the slipped stitch from the needle on the right to that on the left (120 stitches left). To tighten the strands, pull them together.

Lower Border

The 2 x 2 rib stitch across 8 rows will be used to work the lower border

6. Round 1: *Knit 2, Purl 2* to end.
7. Round 1 should be repeated 7 times more.

Note: Fewer or more rounds should be worked if you wish for the border to be shorter or longer

Main Body

The cowl's body is knit in a cable pattern.

Change to bigger needles:

8. Round 1: *C2B, P2, C2F, Purl 2* to end.
9. Round 2: *Knit 2, Purl 2* to end.
10. Rounds 1 and 2 should be repeated until the piece has a measurement of approximately 25cm (9.8 inches) from the cast-on edge or your preferred height. Finish with round 1.

Upper Border

The 2 x 2 rib stitch across 8 rows will be used to work the upper border

Change to shorter needles:
    11. Round 1: *Knit 2, Purl 2* to end.
    12. Round 1 should be repeated 7 times more.

Note: Fewer or more rounds should be worked if you wish for the border to be shorter or longer

Binding Off

Stitches in pattern should be bound off (knit over knit stitches, purl over purl stitches).

13. Knit 2, bringing the first stitch over the second.
14. Knit the next stitch, bringing the first stitch over the second.
15. Rep step 14 till there's 1 stitch remaining; clip the yarn and leave about 4–6 inches tail to weave in later. Pull the yarn tail tight through the last stitch.

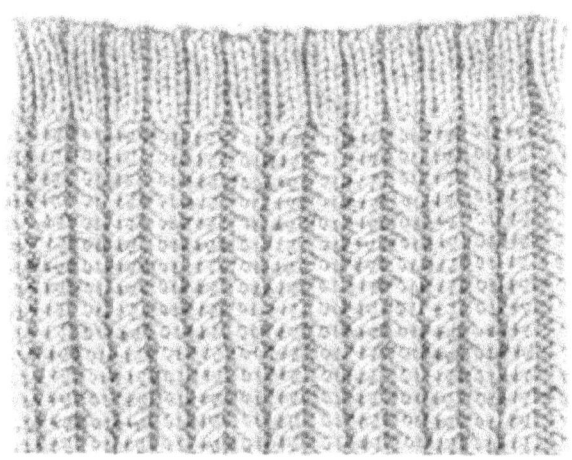

Finishing

16. All loose ends should be weaved in.
17. Block your piece. I usually recommend damp or steam blocking the completed piece since it alters the stitches, making them appear smoother and neater. To do this, simply;
18. Have the knitted piece soaked in lukewarm water for about 10-15 min with some soak wash. Remove it from the water and squeeze off the extra water. After that, place it on a clean towel (ensure no color is transferred), rolling it up to eliminate moisture.
19. Allow the piece to dry by pinning it to a blocking board or laying it on a clean, dry towel (ensure

no color is transferred). After this, your knitting will look much nicer.

Mug Cozy

Tools and Materials

- Worsted weight yarn
- A circular needle or DPNs of US 7 32"
- Tape measure
- Scrap yarn
- Darning/ tapestry needle
- Mug

Measurement

Finished Size:

Circumference = 12 inches

Height = 4¼ inches

Height of handle = 2½ inches

Gauge

- 18 sts x 28 rows = 4 inches

Steps

Before you begin, measure the circumference, height, and height of your handle's cup, which should have straight edges and minimal curves.

Starting the Cozy

1. Cast on 52 stitches and join in the round, then knit.
2. 4 rounds should be worked using the garter stitch, but first, begin with a purl round.

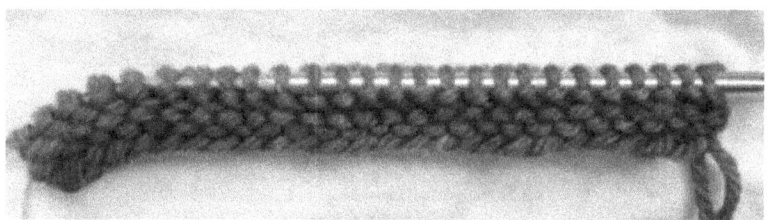

3. Row 5 (Wrong Side): Purl 2, p2tog, purl to 4 stitches from end, p2tog, purl to end.
4. Row 6 (Right Side): Knit.
5. The cozy of the mug should be worked in stockinette stitch until it has a measurement of around 1 row more than 2 inches, finishing on a wrong side row.

Knitting the Space for the Handle

6. Next row: Knit 2, m1L, knit to 2 stitches from end, m1R, knit to end.
7. Next row: Purl.
8. Next row: Knit to the end of the row, then join in the round and knit.
9. 3 rounds of garter stitch should be worked, starting with a purl round.
10. Complete by binding off all stitches. Weave the ends in

Finishing the Mug Cozy

11. Add some finishing touches to your cozy. Use scrap yarn in threading a darning or tapestry needle, using duplicate stitch to create a heart, flower, initials, or whatever you wish!

Customizing Your Mug Cozy Size

- Subtract 1 ¼" from the mug's height to determine the width of your cozy.
- After double-checking your gauge, enough stitches should be cast on to make a circumference of around ½ - 1" lesser than the mug's circumference.
- Work in the round for about ½ inches with your desired edging. Then to accommodate the handle for the mug, you should work in rows while you decrease two stitches on the first row.
- Continue working evenly till the flat piece is the same height as your handle. Work in the round once more after increasing two stitches.

- Note: If your mug has a pretty tall handle, the whole cozy should be worked flat, adding a button or other enclosure to keep it snug.
- Continue in this manner until your cozy reaches the desired width. Finish by binding off and weaving in the ends.

Mittens

Tools and Materials

- 5mm and 6mm DPNs
- Soft, bulky wool yarn in light grey color.
- Stitch marker
- Stitch holder
- Tapestry needle

Measurements

Finished Size:

See below

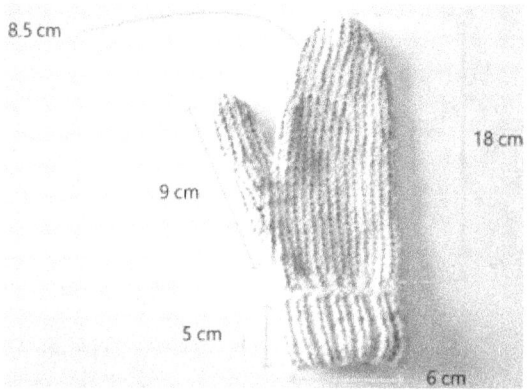

8.5 cm

18 cm

9 cm

5 cm

6 cm

Steps

The Cuff

1. Cast on 30 stitches with 3 5mm DPNs (10 stitches for each needle).

    Some stitches can be added here to accommodate a larger wrist. The best way to modify the number of stitches on every needle throughout the design is for an even number and a multiple of three to be added.

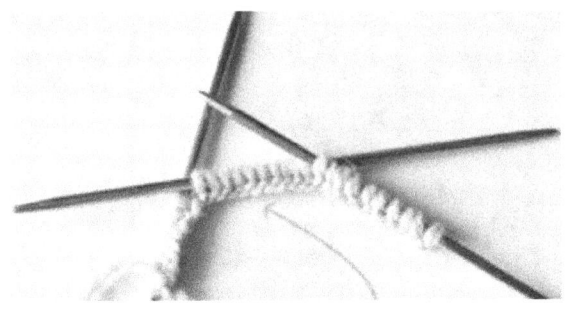

2. Knit 1, Purl 1 for 10cm (22rows). Stitch markers make it simpler to recall where my round begins and ends when knitting in the round for a set amount of rows.

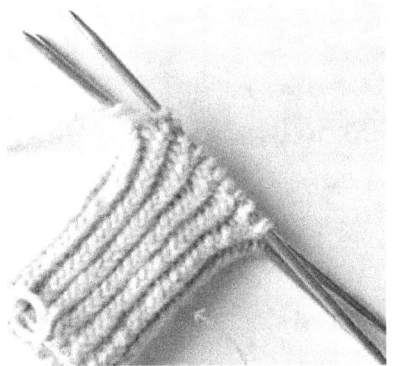

Doesn't it appear to be quite small? Don't worry, the ribs are really elastic and will expand over time.

Still not persuaded? Simply put it on. Place your hand inside the cuff to examine its fitness.

The Thumb

We will make a few increases to provide space for your palm. Now, use 3 6mm DPNs with 4 rounds of knitting.

The increases for the thumb are as follows:

3. On the 1st needle: Knit two stitches in the first stitch; knit 1, and knit two stitches in the third stitch. The remaining 7 stitches should be knitted on the needle. This needle currently has 12 stitches on it.
4. All stitches should be knitted on needles 2 and 3
   - knit 2 rounds
   - increase again
5. On the 1st needle: 2 stitches should be knitted in the first stitch; knit 3, and knit 2 stitches in the fifth stitch. The remaining 7 stitches should be knitted on the needle. This needle now has 14 stitches
6. All stitches should be knitted on needles 2 and 3

5 increases for the tumb

7. 1 round should be knitted

   Increase once more:

   - On the 1st needle: 2 stitches should be knitted
     on the first stitch; knit 5 and knit 2 stitches on
     the 7th stitch. The remaining 7 stitches should
     be knitted on the needle. This needle currently
     has 16 stitches on it.

8. All stitches should be knitted on needles 2 and 3

9. 2 rounds should be knitted

   Increase it once more:

   - On the 1st needle: 2 stitches should be knitted
     on the first stitch; 2 stitches should be knitted
     on 9th stitch. The remaining 7 stitches should
     be knitted on the needle. This needle currently
     has 18 stitches on it.

10. All stitches should be knitted on needles 2 and 3

11. 2 round should be knitted
12. Increase it for the last time:
    - On the 1st needle: 2 stitches should be knitted on the first stitch; knit 5 and knit 2 stitches on the 11th stitch. The remaining 7 stitches should be knitted on the needle. This needle currently has 20 stitches on it.
13. All stitches should be knitted on needles 2 and 3.
14. 3 stitches should be increased at the last round's end (on needle 3).
15. The first needle's 13 stitches should be placed on a stitch holder. These are the thumb's stitches. We'll revisit them later.

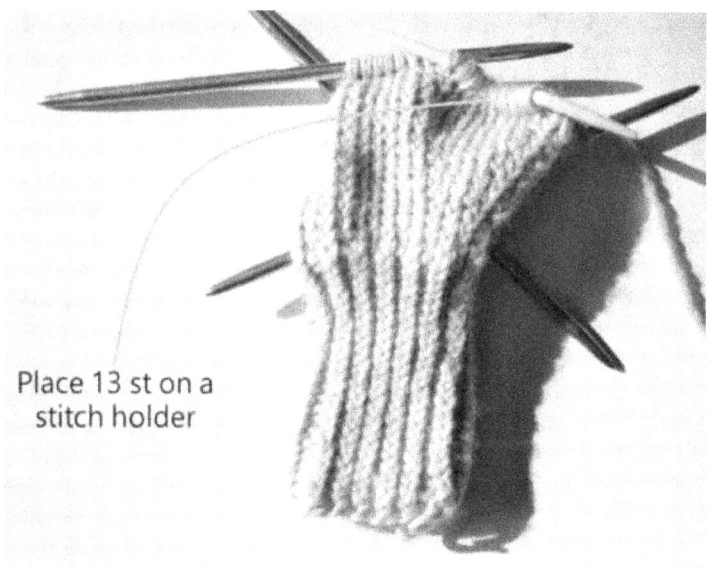

Place 13 st on a stitch holder

Once again, there 30 stitches on the needles and 13 stitches on the needle holder.

The Palm

9 rounds should be knitted

Note: This is where some rounds should be added if your hands are longer. Simply place your hand in the mitten's unfinished portion. The mitten should get to the beginning of your fingers

16. Replace the needles with 4 6mm DPNs. On the needles, the stitches should be divided as given below:
    - Needle 1: 4 stitches (the 3 stitches you introduced at the previous section's end + 1 stitch from the first needle)
    - Needle 2: 11 stitches
    - Needle 3: 4 stitches
    - Needle 4: 11 stitches

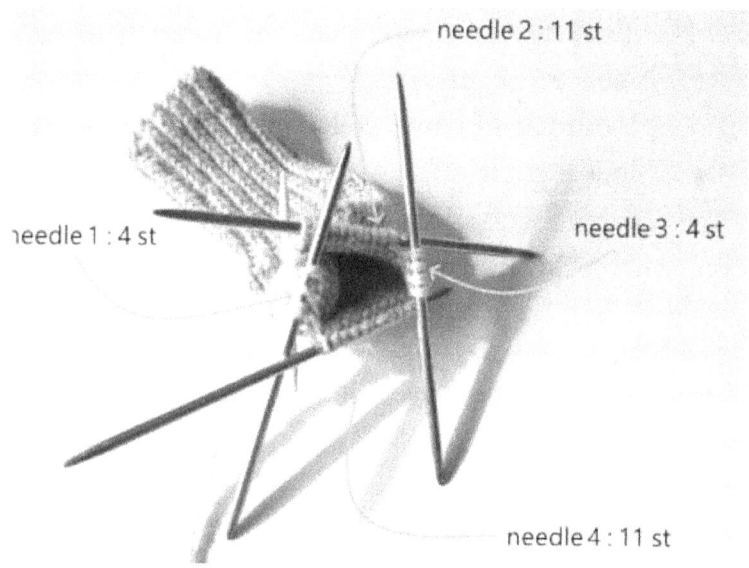

needle 2 : 11 st

needle 1 : 4 st

needle 3 : 4 st

needle 4 : 11 st

17. Next round:
   - Needle 1: knit 1 (the 3 other stitches are from the previous round)
   - Needle 2: ssk, knit 7, k2tog
   - Needle 3: knit 44
   - Needle 4: ssk, knit 7, k2tog
18. 5 rounds should be knitted
19. Next round:
   - Needle 1: knit1, k2tog, knit1
   - Needle 2: All 9 stitches should be knitted
   - Needle 3: knit1, k2tog, knit1
   - Needle 4: All 9 stitches should be knitted
20. 3 rounds should be knitted

21. Next round:
    - Needle 1: knit 3
    - Needle 2: ssk, knit 5, k2tog
    - Needle 3: knit 3
    - Needle 4: ssk, knit 5, k2tog
22. 4 rounds should be knitted

23. The yarn should be passed via all the stitches using a needle.

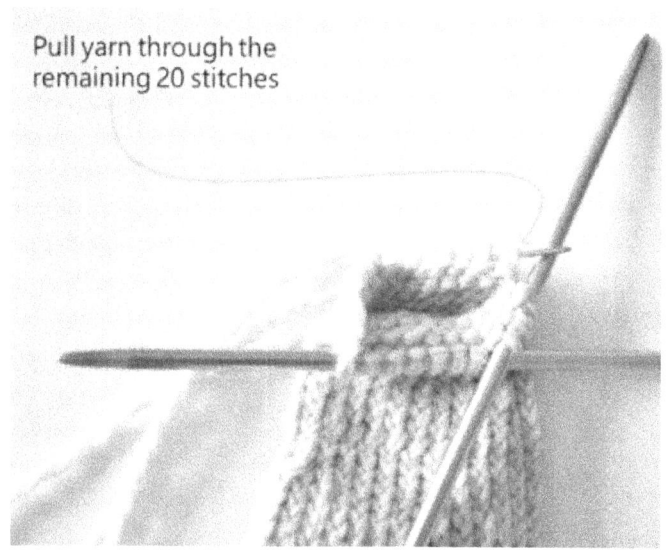

Pull yarn through the remaining 20 stitches

24. Pull the hole tight. I prefer weaving in this tail right away, so there aren't many finishing touches left at the end of the mitten. If you like, you can put it off until later.

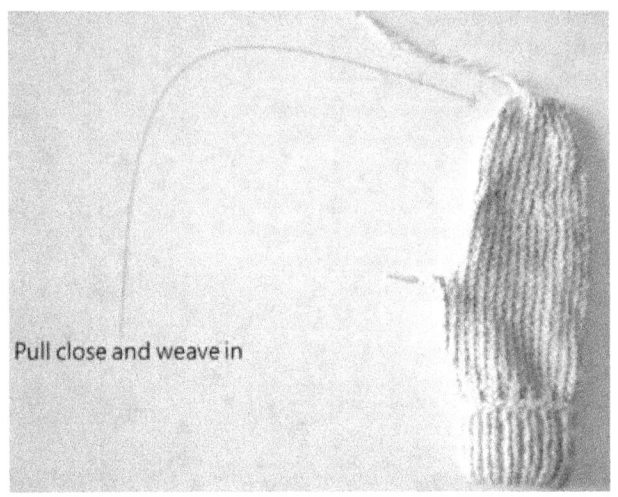

Pull close and weave in

Return to the Thumb

25. Grab the 13 stitches you kept away earlier plus 5
more stitches with 3 6mm DPNs. 6 stitches should
be placed on each of the needles. It makes no
difference how you divide them.

Pick up 5 stitches and
place 6 stitches on each needle

26. 2 rounds should be knitted
27. On each needle: Knit2, k2tog, knit 2
28. 1 round should be knitted
29. On each needle: K2tog, knit3
30. 9 rounds should be knitted

Note: This is where some rounds should be added to adjust the pattern to size if your thumbs are longer. Simply place your hand in the mitten's unfinished portion to know the number of rounds needed.

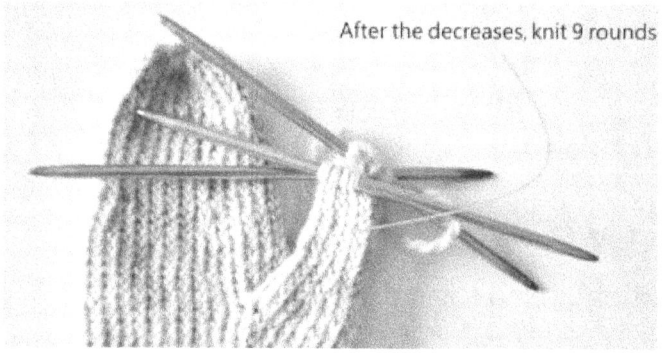

After the decreases, knit 9 rounds

31. The yarn should be pulled tight across all the stitches.
32. Weave all the ends in

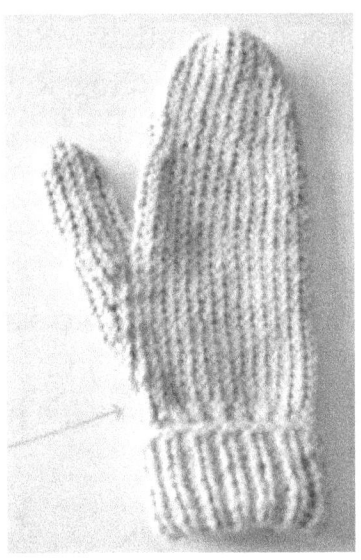

33. Repeat the procedure for the second mitten (upper part of the pattern)

Blocking

I slightly blocked the mittens to make them appear finer and more consistent. Although blocking is not required for this project, it never hurts and can always enhance the look of your mittens.

Conclusion

We've conclusively gotten to the end of this excellent read. Thumbs up if you made it to this section without skipping any chapter, and there is no doubt that you would successfully implement all that has been discussed in the pages of this book.

Knitting generally adds immense value to your health; it can serve as a form of stress relief, build your hand muscles, and improve your hand-to-eye coordination, and circular knitting is not exempted from this. You can also transform your knitted crafts from being a hobby into an actual business that you can sell for some cool cash; isn't that just lovely! The more reason why you must push yourself daily until you master the art of knitting beautiful pieces in the round.

Several learning points were deeply addressed throughout this book to get you started on knitting projects in the round; we touched on the tools and accessories required for circular knitting and provided you a pointer to making the best choice for your needles and yarn, most especially. We also covered some knitting stitches needed for each project that was created. Knitting tips, techniques, and how to resolve common circular knitting problems were discussed in-depth, not to mention the 5 sample projects to jumpstart you into being an expert in knitting projects in the round. I am confident you are well equipped to take the bull by the horn in creating even more advanced projects without much hassle, owing to the knowledge you have gotten from this book. I must say that you will make several mistakes depending on your general experience in knitting but even if you do, ensure you do not throw in the towel, but that you pick up from your mistakes and keep pushing until you get it right. Consistency is key!

What more can I say? I guess I have said all there is to say.

I wish you all the best, knitters!